Granada
and the Alhambra

TEXT
Rafael Hierro Calleja

TRANSLATION
Babel Traducciones, S.L.
(Nicola Jane Graham)

PHOTOGRAPHS
Ángel Sánchez. - Miguel Sánchez
Javier Algarra - Guido Montañés - J. Voigtländer

Ediciones Miguel Sánchez

I would like to dedicate this book to the memory of loved ones who have passed away and the people that have helped me to overcome my sadness and loneliness.

To Pepe Villegas, my colleague and friend for thirty-three years, to my brother Eduardo and my mother Claudia D. Lamberti.

To my sons Ignacio and Daniel, my sister-in-law Concha, Pepi Muñoz, María Estrella Ubiña, María Díaz de la Guardia, Emilio Fuentes and Manuel López Guadalupe, to thank them for their help and support.

I would also like to dedicate this book to all my colleagues at the Asociación Provincial de Intérpretes Turísticos [Provincial Association of Tourist Interpreters] of Granada, for their friendship and understanding. And to the members of the publishing house Ediciones Miguel Sánchez who have made this project possible.

Lastly, and why not? To a wonderful dog that was my companion for twelve years, Koki.

Rafael Hierro

© **Ediciones Miguel Sánchez:** Marqués de Mondéjar, 44. Granada
Text: Rafael Hierro Calleja
Translation: Babel Traducciones, S.L. (Nicola Jane Graham)
Photographs: Ángel Sánchez, Miguel Sánchez, Javier Algarra, Guido Montañés and J. Voigtländer
Checking and coordination: Editorial team at Ediciones Miguel Sánchez
Text on geometrical motifs (Decoration and Ornamentation II): Antonio Marín
Design and layout: Paqui Robles (Bitono)
Typesetting: Paqui Robles and Yasmina Jiménez (Bitono)
City maps: Antonio Marín
Drawings of the Nasrid Palaces and the Generalife: Antonio Mesamadero
Map of the Province: Pilar Campos Fernández Fígares
Photomechanics: Panalitos, S.L. (Granada)
Printing: Grefol, S.L., Móstoles (Madrid)

ISBN: 84-7169-085-3
Depósito legal: GR - 225 / 2005

Table of Contents

The Monasteries of Cartuja and San Jerónimo

Other places of interest

The Province

Guide presentation and contents

Whether you are a traveller or live in the province, you will be well rewarded if you decide to visit, explore and discover Granada. This book, **Granada and the Alhambra**, has been written to accompany not only travellers on their journey through our land, but also residents in Granada who want to find out more about our Art or History, so that they can fully appreciate the images they set eyes on every day.

Perhaps when you look at something you are not aware of its past, you do not see the details, you have not chosen the best perspective, time, day or season. Our aim with this book is to help you see and understand better what you are looking at. For that reason we have provided our readers with itineraries through the city, the Alhambra and the province, all explained in six chapters. A general map and area maps will help you find your way around. Several monographs inserted into the chapters provide more details on the techniques of Muslim decoration and on some important figures that had an influence on Granadine history.

The chapter on **The Alhambra** provides information on and explores the most emblematic monument in the city, taking up more than a third of this book. The history of the Muslims and the Christian intervention are combined with an extremely detailed account of their gardens and architecture.

From the hill of the Alhambra you cross over to the hill where the **Albaycin** stands. The pages in this chapter describe the Lower Albaycin, Sacromonte and the Upper Albaycin by means of itineraries along narrow and steep streets, dotted with singular buildings. There is a series of *carmens* (houses with a small orchard) and miradors, as well as an unforgettable view of the majestic Alhambra and the valley of the River Darro separating the two hills.

In the next chapter, we go down to the flat part of Granada to visit **The Cathedral and its Surroundings**. The text and the photographs complement each other perfectly to help us explore this diverse and spectacular complex, with special attention paid to its two architectural jewels: the Cathedral and the Royal Chapel. But there are also many other places and monuments to discover, such as the Alcaiceria (Muslim trading quarter), the Madraza (Arab university), the Corral del Carbon (formerly the Muslim Corn Exchange), the square called Plaza Bibarrambla, etc. This is the heart of 21st century Granada, flanked by history on all sides.

Another chapter has been set aside to describe the numerous Churches and Monasteries spread out in the north-west: **The Monasteries of Cartuja and San Jerónimo**. Although the Monastery of Cartuja is further removed from the Cathedral environment, the majority of the other religious and civil monuments described are no more than five hundred metres from the Cathedral, so they can all be visited in less than half a day.

There are other places in the city, not included in the preceding chapters, which you should try to see if you have time. They are described in **Other Places of Interest**, which also includes, as a special inclusion, a selection of the most interesting museums and house-museums in Granada.

And the end of our journey with our readers opens the door to **The Province**. The images on these pages are an invitation to enjoy the landscape, the light and the peace and quiet of Granada's countryside, which is well worth planning a special visit to.

Lastly, as the editors, we hope this book helps to make your discovery of Granada something you will never forget.

The editorial team

"The Surrender of Granada". Painter: Pradilla.

Some history

At the very beginning, the lands of the city and province of Granada were inhabited by Iberian tribes, evidenced by the discovery of "the Lady of Baza", the finest example of Iberian art. Later, the Phoenicians founded the colonies of "Salubinia" (Salobreña) and "Sexi" (Almuñécar) on the coast. There are not many traces of Greek culture, but the Romans certainly left their mark. Apparently, there was a settlement called Eliberris (Ilíberis – Ilbira – Elvira) here first, located in the valley of the River Darro, on the hill where the Albaycin is today, which the entire region was named after. When Ilíberis was christianised by St. Cecilius in the 1st century, an Episcopal see was founded in it and the "Council of Elvira" was held there in the 4th century, the first one to take place on the peninsula. When the Muslims conquered the peninsula, there were three important population centres in the area: two Roman-Gothic ones, the above-mentioned "Ilíberis" and "Castilia", at the foot of Sierra Elvira, and a third Jewish one, "Garnatha Alyehud", at the foot of the *Torres Bermejas* (Red Towers), which was really the poor quarter of Ilíberis. The Muslims occupied Castilia first, calling it "Medina Ilbira" (Medina Elvira), the capital of Elvira, and they called the neighbouring population centre, on the hill of the River Darro, Granada. At the beginning of the 11th century, Zawi Ibn Zirí moved his court and the capital of his kingdom, which had been in Medina Elvira, to the hill where the Albaycin is today, which is where the former Ilíberis stood. This is the moment when the city of Granada came into being as far as history is concerned.

A great deal can be written about the years when the Muslim peoples occupied the Iberian peninsula, as this spanned almost eight centuries. However, as far as the history of Granada is concerned, there are two very specific periods worth emphasising, which were ruled over by two dynasties: the Zirid dynasty (1013–1090) and the Nasrid dynasty (1238–1492). The Zirids because they built the city and founded it as an independent kingdom. The Nasrids because they were the last reigning Muslim monarchy in Spain, with their most precious jewel, the city of Granada, as their capital. In the medieval Nasrid period the city also expanded and grew as never before.

The Nasrid Kingdom of Granada, with a population of over 400,000, covered an area from Cabo de Gata to Gibraltar, including the current provinces of Almeria, Granada, Malaga, part of Cadiz and Jaen. Nasrid Granada was not a dominating and strong empire as Cordoba was. It was a kingdom that had been encircled. From the start, it had had to pay taxes to the powerful Castilian crown and, aware of its weakness, it always looked for support against its enemies in friendship. Paradoxically, and as a counterpoint to this military weakness, the kingdom of Granada was strong intellectually and culturally, the home to many great poets, artists and thinkers. During this period, the city expanded and grew more than ever before as Muslims from Úbeda, Baeza, Antequera and other localities came to settle here, swelling the number of inhabitants to around 50,000. Not only did they build the Alhambra, but also mosques, palaces, hospitals and even a University.

The Christian era began with the conquest of Granada by the Catholic Monarchs on 2 January 1492, bringing with it a new age of splendour. The new Christian monarchs completely pampered the city, as the conquest marked the end of the long period of the Reconquest. A large number of churches, convents and monasteries were built in Granada to reassert the triumph of the Catholic religion over Islam. In those first years of the reigns of the Catholic Monarchs and of Emperor Charles V the city's great Christian monuments were built: Royal Chapel, Cathedral, Convent of Santa Isabel la Real (St. Isabella the Royal), University, Palace of Charles V, Monastery of San Jerónimo (St. Jerome), etc., which are late Gothic and Renaissance in style. Artists as important as Egás, Siloé and Machuca came to work in Granada in this period.

Although the victorious Christians, Jews and Moriscos[1] were able to live together in the first few years after the conquest, the victors' ideological positions became more radical as time went by, further limiting the rights that had at first been granted to people with other faiths. There was far more intolerance shown towards Jews, who were expelled, than towards Moriscos, who were tolerated. Nevertheless, at the end of the 16th century, when Philip II was on the throne, the Moriscos' rights were totally violated and they were plagued by taxes and more intolerance towards their customs, which came to a head in the bloody "Morisco Rebellion" or "War of the

Alpujarras" (1568-1571). The Moriscos were defeated and later, during the reign of Philip III, they were expelled. This led to an enormous setback in the economy, agriculture and craftwork at a national level, but above all in Granada, due to the huge enriching influence they had here.

The Baroque and Post Baroque of the 17th and 18th centuries marked another prosperous time for Granada's architecture, as this was when monuments such as the Monastery of Cartuja (completed), the Basilicas of San Juan de Dios (St. John of God) and Virgen de las Angustias (Our Lady of Sorrows) and the Church of Sagrario (Tabernacle) were built. There was another group of great artists, who created a school within and outside the city: Alonso Cano, Pedro de Mena, José Risueño, the Moras....

There was a decline at the start of the 19th century with the Napoleonic invasion, which destroyed part of the city's wealth of monuments. In 1829, the American writer Washington Irving came to Granada and he wrote the "Tales of the Alhambra". The city made a comeback, as many writers, artists and romantic travellers came here, attracted by its legends: Dumas, Daumier, Delacroix, David Roberts..., who immortalised the city and gave it a universal dimension.

Granada experienced a new boom with Isabella II's visit in 1862 and the coronation of the poet José Zorrilla in the Palace of Charles V in 1889, and measures were taken to restore the Alhambra, which finally opened its doors to the public in the reign of Alfonso XIII. Since then to our times, Granada's fame has spread, especially during the "Generation of 27" with Federico García Lorca, Manuel de Falla, Pablo Neruda, Salvador Dalí and Juan Ramón Jiménez, who turned it into one of the most important artistic, literary and musical cities, not just in Spain, but in the world.

[1] At the beginning, the Catholic Monarchs agreed to respect the religious practices of the defeated Muslims, who in exchange paid a tax. Nevertheless, not much later, they were forced to adopt the Catholic religion. These new Christians, recently baptised Muslims converted to Christianity, were known as *Moriscos*. When they were baptised, they were given Christian names, although in the majority of the cases their Christianity was only apparent, since they continued to live their lives following Muslim customs.

The Alhambra

MAP OF THE ALHAMBRA AND

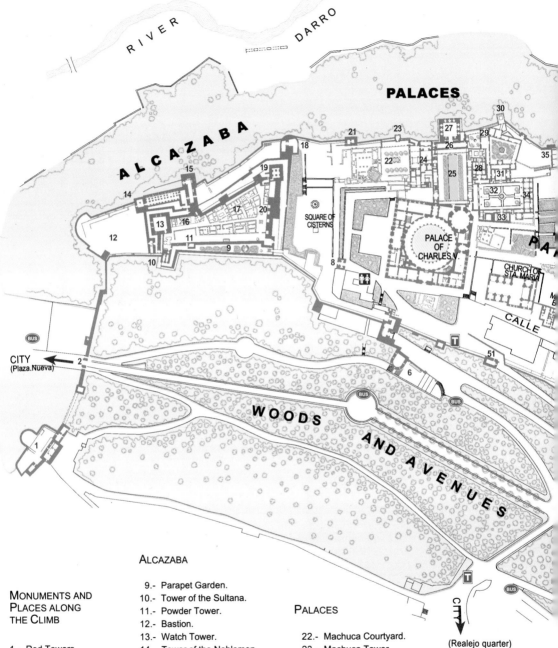

PALACES

ALCAZABA

PALACES

RIVER DARRO

SQUARE OF CISTERNS

PALACE OF CHARLES V.

CHURCH OF STA. MARIA

CALLE

WOODS AND AVENUES

CITY (Plaza Nueva)

(Realejo quarter)

BUS

THE GENERALIFE

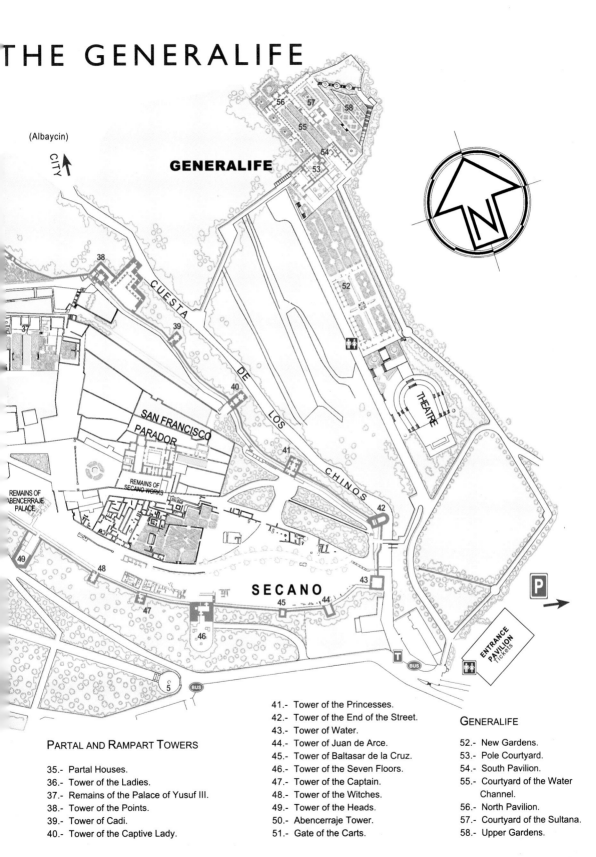

(Albaycin)

CITY

GENERALIFE

GENERALIFE

CUESTA DE LOS CHINOS

THEATRE

SAN FRANCISCO PARADOR

REMAINS OF SECANO WORKS

REMAINS OF ABENCERRAJE PALACE

SECANO

ENTRANCE PAVILION Tickets

BUS

BUS

PARTAL AND RAMPART TOWERS

35.- Partal Houses.
36.- Tower of the Ladies.
37.- Remains of the Palace of Yusuf III.
38.- Tower of the Points.
39.- Tower of Cadi.
40.- Tower of the Captive Lady.

41.- Tower of the Princesses.
42.- Tower of the End of the Street.
43.- Tower of Water.
44.- Tower of Juan de Arce.
45.- Tower of Baltasar de la Cruz.
46.- Tower of the Seven Floors.
47.- Tower of the Captain.
48.- Tower of the Witches.
49.- Tower of the Heads.
50.- Abencerraje Tower.
51.- Gate of the Carts.

GENERALIFE

52.- New Gardens.
53.- Pole Courtyard.
54.- South Pavilion.
55.- Courtyard of the Water Channel.
56.- North Pavilion.
57.- Courtyard of the Sultana.
58.- Upper Gardens.

Location of the monument's different areas: the route followed in the book

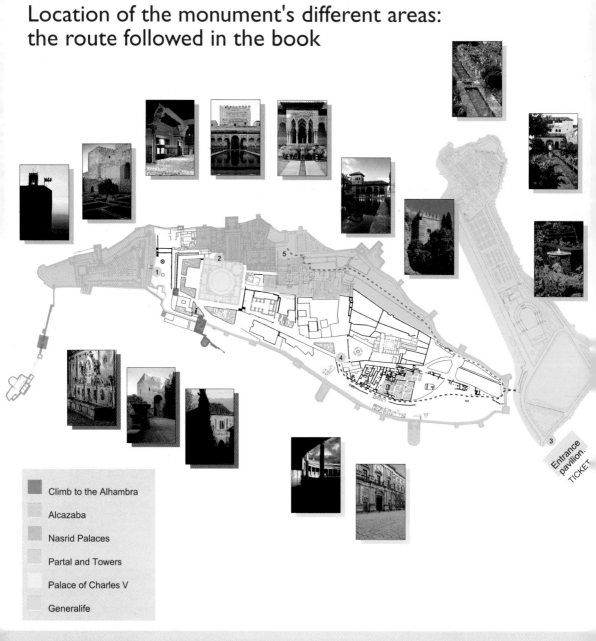

Climb to the Alhambra

Alcazaba

Nasrid Palaces

Partal and Towers

Palace of Charles V

Generalife

INFORMATION OF INTEREST:
The entrance ticket gives you access to the monument's three independent areas.

1.- ALCAZABA: Accessed from the western side of the **Plaza de los Aljibes** (Square of Cisterns) (no. 1), the open area next to the Puerta del (Gate of Wine).

2.- PALACES: The entrance is opposite the northern side of the **Palace of Charles V** (no. 2). The Partal and the Towers are next to the Palace you exit.
    * The entrance time for this area of the monument is stated on the ticket.

3.- GENERALIFE: There are several possible accesses. The main entrance is next to the **Entrance Pavilion** (no. 3); it can also be accessed from control point next to the Parador de San Francisco, crossing the Secano (no. 4); lastly, walking along the avenue that runs between the **Partal** **the Towers** (no. 5), at the end of it.

▪▪▪▪▪▪▪▪▪▪▪▪▪▪▪▪▪▪▪▪▪▪▪▪▪▪▪▪▪▪ **Secano Walkway**
▪▪▪▪▪▪▪▪▪▪▪▪▪▪▪▪▪▪▪▪▪▪▪▪▪▪▪▪▪▪ **Avenue of the Partal and the Towers**

The Alhambra seen from the Albaycin.

Introduction

The Alhambra was a real walled "city", built by the Nasrid Kings in the last period of Muslim rule in Spain.

Coat of arms of the Nasrid Kings.

Nearly everyone who comes to Granada and visits the Alhambra for the first time asks the same questions: What does Alhambra mean, what it is, who had it built, why...? And there are even more questions when they go inside and start to wander around the marvels of this monument, amazed by its beauty and a little lost. That is why the pages of a good book are needed to help you find the answers to these and the many other questions you may have.

The name *Alhambra* comes from the Arabic word *qalat-al-hamrá*, which means "red", "red castle" or "reddish". A first theory about this meaning would be based on the reddish colour of the ferruginous materials used to build it, mainly adobe bricks. However, it is now thought that the walls of the Alhambra were white, like the walls of the Generalife or the houses in the Albaycin, and that the red colour, as narrated by the Arab chronicler, Ibn Aljatib, comes from the gleam of the torches when night fell, giving the walls this special colour. It was the inhabitants of the neighbouring quarter of the Albaycin and of the Vega (fertile plain) who gave it this name.

The purpose of this introduction is to give some initial information before starting your visit, which will help you to understand this complex of monuments, this "jewel" of Arab architecture, which was built by the Nasrid Emirs of the Kingdom of Granada in the last period of history of Muslin rule on the Peninsula. And fundamental for your

understanding is knowing a little about the history of the reign of the Muslim peoples in Spain and Granada, as well as finding out about what the space enclosed by the Alhambra's ramparts actually contained. This is the only way you can understand what it really was, a true palatine city, especially as only thirty percent of its constructions and palaces have survived to this day.

THE SPANISH MUSLIMS, RULERS OF AL-ÁNDALUS (711-1492)

The conquest by the Muslims of Al-Ándalus, which is what they called Spain, was fast and easy. At the beginning of the 8th century, the Visigoth reign of Spain had been greatly weakened by corruption and the fighting of its governors, which meant that the Muslims from the other side of the Straits of Gibraltar were able to occupy the lands very rapidly. The existing communities of Christians and Jews were tolerated in exchange for taxes, so the population of Al-Ándalus was a mixture of races and creeds.

A priori, it would be difficult to understand why the Muslim peoples, for whom the *jihad*, "holy war", is one of their fundamental religious precepts, allowed other religions to coexist in the towns they occupied. The explanation lies in the fact that the Jewish and Christian religions were also monotheist, related to Islam through *Abraham* (the father of the three religions). Moreover, for the Muslims, Jews and Christians were "brothers" who had made a mistake and who did not want to accept Allah's message. The Muslims called the Christians and the Jews *Ahl-al-kitab*, which means "book people", referring to the Bible, which they even took part of their traditions and previous revelations from. That is the reason why they were granted a special status.

But if there is anything that characterised the Muslims' reign in Al-Ándalus, it was the fragmentation and fragility of their territories, which meant that their rule was never peaceful. These were times of constant wars, either against the Christians, who were gradually narrowing the siege to the north, or against other Muslims,

The Alhambra and Sierra Nevada.

sometimes even those from Al-Ándalus, other times tribes from the north of Africa, who were constantly invading them from the south. This circumstance meant that the rulers had to resort to policies of pacts and alliances to keep the peace in their territories. The Muslim rule of Al-Ándalus and Granada had several different periods:

– THE DEPENDENT EMIRATE (711-756): In 711, seven thousand Muslim warriors, most of them Berbers, led by Tariq Ibn Ziyad, crossed the Straits of Gibraltar and defeated Don Rodrigo (a Visigoth king) near Algeciras. This was to be the first of many other victories leading to a rapid Islamisation of the country. In this first period, the territories conquered were ruled by governors who reported directly to the Caliph of Damascus.

– THE INDEPENDENT EMIRATE (756-929): This period started with the figure of Abd-al-Rahman I (from the Omeya dynasty), who

disembarked in Almuñécar, on the Granadine coast, took over Seville and defeated the emir of Al-Ándalus near Cordoba, thus establishing the independent emirate. Abd-al-Rahman I governed as an independent sovereign without having to account to anybody, creating an organised and prosperous State that lasted almost 200 years.

– THE CALIPHATE (929-1013): This started with Abd-al-Rahman III, who proclaimed himself caliph and prince of believers and established the Caliphate of Cordoba. This was the time when Cordoba was at its most splendid and Granada remained in the background, submissive to the Caliphate.

– TAIFA KINGDOMS-THE ZIRID KINGDOM OF GRANADA (1013-1090): When the Omeyas and the Caliphate of Cordoba collapsed at the beginning of the 11th century, Al-Ándalus was divided into tiny kingdoms or governments called

"*Taifa kingdoms*", each one ruled by a family or dynasty, which often fought each other. The *Zirids* settled in Granada. There were four kings in this dynasty. Under their rule, the capital status of Elvira was transferred to Granada, which started as a kingdom with these kings.

– THE ALMORAVIDS AND ALMOHADS (1090-1231): This period can be classified as the *Berber rule*, bringing with it more religious fanaticism and cultural regression. The *Almoravids* were Berbers from the desert and recent converts to Islam. They entered Al-Ándalus, which had been much weakened by the constant fights between the Andalusian Taifa emirs, from the north of Africa and swept the *Zirids* impetuously aside. History was to repeat itself, and another new tribe of Berbers from the north of Africa appeared, the *Almohads,* who ruled Muslim Spain until the first third of the 13th century.

This century was to mark the decline of Muslims in Spain (Al-Ándalus), whose control was reduced by the powerful actions of Castile and Aragon. All this was aggravated by their constant internal divisions, caused by the personal ambitions of their kings, a problem that always undermined the power of the Hispano-Arabs.

– THE NASRIDS OF THE KINGDOM OF GRANADA (1238-1492): This was the last reigning Muslim dynasty in Spain and it arose around the *Nasar or Nasrid* family, who lived in Arjona. Most noteworthy among them is the figure of *Muhammad* (called *Ibn Yusuf Ibn Nasr Ibn al-Ahmar*) who was the great opportunist of that age of unrest and combat, when more or less improvised leaders aspired to dominate the country. After different victories in a series of territories, *Alhamar* became more and more popular among the Muslims, possibly even more so as a result of the gradual defeats his rivals suffered, as the Christians gradually reconquered territories.

A determining factor was the loss of Cordoba by Ibn Hud (his most direct Muslim rival) to King Ferdinand's Christian troops. That caused the Granadines, who had been previously reluctant to do so, to decide to recognise Muhammad from Arjona as their emir, since they needed a lord and master to obey and to direct their lives.

Muhammad, also known as *al-Ahmar, the magnificent*, made his entrance into the great city of Granada in the holy month of Ramadan in the year 1238. And that date, for chronological purposes, is the one considered as the beginning of the Nasrid kingdom in Granada. This kingdom, the last of Muslim Spain, included the current complete provinces of Granada, Malaga and Almeria and part of Jaen, Cordoba, Seville and Cadiz.

Muhammad I (al-Ahmar) proclaimed himself a vassal and ally of King Ferdinand III of Castile and thus assured Granada's stability and permanence. Vassalage consisted of paying an annual tax of 150,000 gold maravedis and helping him in any of his military campaigns with a hundred and fifty lancers. Having achieved peace, the population of Granada trebled, industry grew and the arts and sciences were promoted. But, without a doubt, Muhammad I's most extraordinary achievement was the fact that he was the one responsible for starting the construction of the ALHAMBRA, which his descendants enlarged. The most prominent of them are, above all, Yusuf I and Muhammad V, in the 14th century, the true golden age of the Nasrid reign.

THE HISTORY OF THE ALHAMBRA AND ITS MONARCHS
IN CHRONOLOGICAL ORDER

The first point to note is that the Alhambra was not a residence of kings until the 13th century, since the first Granadine kings, who, as stated above, were the *Zirids*, established their palaces and their strongest defences on the hill opposite, where the *Albaycin* is located, in the 11th century. And all that is left now is our memories of them and the remains of some ramparts. It was the Nasrid kings who established their palaces on *Sabika* hill (where the Alhambra is located) for the first time, where there were already the remains of another military construction, possibly dating from the 9th century.

The Alcazaba. It was built in the reign of Muhammad I (1238-1273).

There is a brief summary below of how the construction of the Alhambra evolved and the role played in building it by the most noteworthy of the monarchs who lived there.

– **MUHAMMAD I, AL-AHMAR (1238-1273):** The founder of the dynasty, with great political skills. He has the honour of being the one that started the construction of the Alhambra as a palace for the Granadine kings. He built the Alcazaba from the remains of the former fortress that already existed on Sabika hill and established his palace in it. He provided it with water from the River Darro by constructing a weir. He was responsible for the Torre de la Vela (Watch Tower) and the Torre del Homenaje (Keep) in the Alcazaba. He improved the defences and created storage areas for grain and ammunition. He probably built the ramparts as well.

Partal Palace. It is attributed to Muhammad III (1302-1309).

– **MUHAMMAD II (1273-1302):** He was a scholarly king of science and a reader of the Koran among his family, which is why the Granadines called him "alfaqui" (*learned man*). He continued the construction of the palace and the walled complex started by his father. It seems that the Torre de las Damas (Tower of the Ladies) and the Torre de los Picos (Tower of the Points), on the north side of the complex, also belong to this period. He may have been the king who started the construction of the Generalife. It may also have been him who built Mexuar Palace (which may even have been started by his father).

Generalife Palace. Ismail I (1314-1325) is considered to be its true builder.

– **MUHAMMAD III (1302-1309):** A blind and dethroned king, which is why he was called "al-majlu" (*the dethroned one*). During his reign there was a generous sense of tolerance: many foreigners came to Granada and Christians married Muslim women. He was responsible for a public bath and the Royal Mosque, on which the Church of Santa Maria was later built and now stands. New studies also attribute the construction of Partal Palace to him, which is the oldest of the Alhambra's palaces.

Mexuar Palace. We cannot be sure who the monarch responsible for building it was. But it is much older than the other two palaces of the Royal Residence.

– **ISMAIL I (1314-1325):** He was an energetic prince, who the Muslim chroniclers paint with all kinds of virtues, including chastity. He extended and redecorated the Generalife. He is usually thought of as its real builder. He defeated the Christians near Sierra Elvira, which is where the princes Don Juan and Don Pedro died. He also won the Plaza de Martos in Jaen.

Comares Palace. It was built during the reign of Yusuf I (1333-1354).

Palace of the Lions. It is the work of Muhammad V (1354-1391).

Tower of the Princesses. This is one of the last constructions built in the Alhambra, which Muhammad VII (1392-1408) was responsible for.

– MUHAMMAD IV (1325-1333): The emir with a tragic destiny: he was assassinated. He may have been responsible for building Mexuar Palace, although it is also logical for it to have been built, at least partly, at the time of Yusuf I.

– YUSUF I (1333-1354): The Kingdom of Granada was at its most splendid during his reign and that of his son. They were responsible for almost all the palaces as they are today. He renovated the Alcazaba, built the Puertas de la Justicia and Armas (Gates of Justice and of Weapons), Comares Palace and the Baths of the Palace. He may have built or rebuilt numerous towers, such as: Siete Suelos (Seven Floors), Cadí, Cautiva (Captive Lady), Machuca and Comares. The most outstanding of them all is the Tower of the Captive Lady, whose rich decoration inside makes it seem like a small palace. He also built the Madraza (university) opposite the Main Mosque in Granada. Among his military merits is that he managed to destroy the Castilian squadron in the waters of the Straits of Gibraltar in 1340 in the largest naval battle of the century. He was assassinated by a madman in the mosque of the Alhambra.

– MUHAMMAD V (1354-1391): The king that governed twice, since power was usurped from him, although he then managed to regain it. He continued his father's work, redecorating some parts of Comares Palace, such as its majestic entrance facade. His greatest contribution was the construction of the Palacio de los Leones (Palace of the Lions), with its well-known courtyard and all the rooms and buildings surrounding it. He also built the "Maristán" hospital in the Albaycin. During his reign, he formed a government of intellectuals, who included the multi-faceted writer Ibn-al-Jatib and the poet Ibn Zamrak. He was a friend of the Christian King Peter I "The Cruel" and he helped him to restore the Royal Alcazares of Seville.

– MUHAMMAD VII (1392-1408): He was a bellicose king who occupied the throne by passing over the rights of his oldest brother, Yusuf, who he ordered to have imprisoned in Salobreña Castle. During his reign, the poet Ibn Zamrak was assassinated. His most important contribution to the Alhambra was the construction of the Torre de las Infantas (Tower of the Princesses), whose interior is one of the most beautiful of all the towers in the complex. Some people attribute the construction of this tower to a later monarch, Saad (1454-1464).

– YUSUF III (1408-1417): He was possibly the last great king of Granada. After him, the Nasrid dynasty entered a period of agony. Before he came to the throne, as already mentioned, he was imprisoned in Salobreña. The chronicles say that when he was there, a letter arrived from his brother Muhammad VII in Granada ordering his execution. Yusuf asked to say farewell to his family and permission was not granted. Then he asked them to let him finish the game of chess he was playing with the governor of the stronghold, which he was allowed to do. Yusuf, sensing that something was going to happen, tried to keep the game going for as long as possible, and before it finished, a group of Granadine noblemen arrived at the castle, freed him and took him to Granada. He was proclaimed king in 1408. He built the palace of Yusuf III in the area we know nowadays as the Upper Partal. Although this palace does not exist as such today, since only ruins remain, it must have been behind the Palaces of Comares and the Lions, the most sumptuous construction of the Alhambra.

The later Nasrid kings who lived in the Alhambra belong to a period we can classify as the "agony and death of the kingdom", filled with civil conflicts and fights against the

Partal Palace as it is today.

Drawing of Partal Palace by Lewis when he visited Granada (1833-1834).

Top right and left: These images give us an idea of the deplorable state of deterioration of some of the rooms in the Alhambra in the 18th and 19th centuries.

Christians, so, apart from the reign of Saad, not much was contributed to the monument. A decline started with them which ended with Boabdil, the last Nasrid king, who officially handed over the city and its strongholds to the Catholic Monarchs, Isabella of Castile and Ferdinand of Aragon, on 2 January 1492.

– THE CHRISTIAN MONARCHS: When the Catholic Monarchs arrived in Granada they occupied the Alcazaba and fortifications and the Royal Nasrid Residence (Mexuar Palace, Comares Palace and Palace of the Lions). The rest of the Alhambra's palaces and residences were divided among their court. The Catholic Monarchs were marvelled by the beauty of these palaces and as a result they preserved them in their entirety, apart from some small modifications to adapt them to their requirements.

The Catholic Monarchs granted the city of the Alhambra its own jurisdiction with the Count of Tendilla as its governor. The Christian inhabitants of this palatine city created a kind of small court that preserved and inhabited the houses and palaces, even adopting many Muslim customs. At the time, the population was formed by a curious mixture of Christians and Moriscos (Muslims who adopted the Catholic religion in order to stay in Spain, in many cases only apparently, as they kept their Muslim traditions and ways of life). Logically, some Christian constructions were also built, such as the *Church of Santa Maria*, on the former site of the Main Mosque. When Charles V went to Granada he also lived here. He had new rooms built in the Royal Residence and ordered the Renaissance palace to be built, which is named after him.

When the Bourbons came to the throne in Spain, the Alhambra fell into disgrace. Its inhabitants had supported the House of Austria in the succession conflict for the crown of Spain, which took place between 1700 and 1713, so they were not exactly appreciated by the new Spanish royal family. With the invasion of Napoleon's French troops, the Alhambra ran a real risk of disappearing altogether. The French troops, the rulers of Granada between 1808 and 1812, converted the palaces into barracks, devastating many of them. Miraculously the palaces of the Royal Residence survived. During their retreat, they mined the towers, destroying part of them. Some of them, such as the Torre de los Sietes Suelos (Tower of the Seven Floors) or Torre del Agua (Tower of Water) were left in ruins.

In the 18th and part of the 19th centuries, the rooms in the abandoned Alhambra were turned into dung heaps and taverns, occupied by the lowest social class of people. This abandonment was reflected in the texts and drawings by many of the travellers that visited Granada at the time, such as Gustavo Doré,

Richard Ford, Prangey, Roberts and Lewis. At last, the Alhambra was declared a national monument in 1870 and since then it has been restored and protected for all to enjoy and admire.

THE ALHAMBRA AS A REAL CITY

Everyone who visits the Alhambra for the first time thinks that it is just the Nasrid Palace, or Royal Residence, with the Patio de los Leones (Courtyard of the Lions) and its rooms as the focal point. But the Alhambra covers a far greater area and was originally a real *palatine city*, like an acropolis, fortified and "isolated" from the city of Granada. It covered an approximate area of 104,000 square metres and had the same characteristic buildings and quarters found in every Muslim city.

The most characteristic types of construction in every Hispano-Muslim city are the following:

– Religious constructions:
Mosques (temples), morabitos (hermitages) and rawdas (cemeteries).

– Civil constructions:
Private homes, alcazares (palaces), madrazas (universities), fondacs (guest houses), fundqs (marketplaces for wheat and other goods) and maristanes (hospitals).

– Military constructions:
Alcazabas (fortresses), towers, access gates to cities and bridges.

Almost all these buildings were in the Alhambra, although over time many of them have disappeared. Only what is left of the Alcazaba, the majority of the towers and the most important palaces have remained. However, in its heyday, the Alhambra was a real walled city, with at least seven palaces, residences for completely diverse social categories, all kinds of offices, the royal mint, private and public mosques, workshops of different trades, shops, public and private baths, a royal cemetery and a fortress with barracks and prisons.

The city was protected by all the towers (there were up to thirty) and the ramparts, which went around the perimeter. There were at least three entrance gates to it: the Puertas de la Justicia and Armas (Gates of Justice and of Weapons), both strongly fortified, in the north-west part and south-west part of the city, for access to the Alcazaba and the Royal Residence. In the south-east sector was the *Puerta de los Siete Suelos* (the Gate of the Seven

Left:
The Alhambra and its towers seen from the Generalife.

THE ALHAMBRA AS A REAL CITY

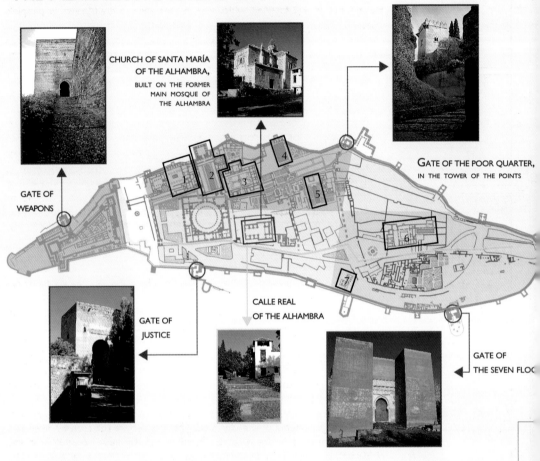

CHURCH OF SANTA MARÍA OF THE ALHAMBRA, BUILT ON THE FORMER MAIN MOSQUE OF THE ALHAMBRA

GATE OF THE POOR QUARTER, IN THE TOWER OF THE POINTS

GATE OF WEAPONS

GATE OF JUSTICE

CALLE REAL OF THE ALHAMBRA

GATE OF THE SEVEN FLOC

Military area, where the garrison in charge of the citadel's security lived.

Residential and palatine area, occupied by the royal family, where the court's official life transpired. Apart from the three palaces forming the Royal Nasrid Residence, there were other palaces and noblemen's houses in this area, which leads us to believe that the most distinguished families in the Alhambra lived here.

Civil area, medina or people's quarter, where the majority of the population lived: officials, servants, craftsmen and other inhabitants, all of them responsible for covering the city's requirements and its smooth operation. It is the most damaged area in the Alhambra, and only some archaeological remains are still left. Due to the amount of remains found, we know that the most populated area, the real medina in the complex, is where you can see a more intense colour on the surface.

Ring road or **parapet walk**: it goes round the entire complex right next to the internal face of the ramparts, going past or below the towers, except in the case of the Torre del Agua (Tower of Water), at the most eastern end, where it separates from the ramparts. The area where this line is broken is where this street crosses the internal part of the palaces.

Calle Real Baja (Lower Royal Street): it crossed the palatine area from one end to the other. The route of this street is correct for part of the way, but in others it is an approximate reconstruction.

Calle Real Alta (Upper Royal Street): it crossed the entire medina, no doubt the longest and the most used street in the entire city. As is the case with Calle Real Baja, the route is an approximation from studies carried out with certain parts that are known to be correct. Part of the route coincides with the current "Calle Real de la Alhambra", although it would probably not have been as straight and wide.

Secondary streets: these are the most difficult to define, although we know that there were some and that they linked the streets Real Alta and Baja. Those marked here are the ones on which different research seems most to agree.

1.- Mexuar Palace

2.- Comares Palace

3.- Palace of the Lions

4.- Partal Palace

5.- Remains of the Palace of Yusu (central pool)

6.- San Francisco Monastery. It built on the remains of a for Arab palace. It is now a Natic Tourism Parador.

7.- Remains of Abencerraje Pala

Floors), not as well fortified, which was the entrance to the Medina, or people's quarter, which is nowadays known as the *Secano* (this area occupied more than half of the complex). According to tradition, Boabdil left the Alhambra through the *Gate of the Seven Floors*. The Catholic Monarchs, out of respect for him, ordered it to be walled up so that no one could ever pass through it again. The *Puerta del Arrabal* (Gate of the Poor Quarter in the Tower of the Points) cannot be considered as one of the citadel's gates as it was an access linking the Alhambra with the Generalife.

There was a university **("Madraza"),** located in the space between the Alcazaba and Machuca Tower. The most important palaces, many of them today left with ruins inside or with only an incomplete part standing, are: the three palaces forming the Royal Residence (*Mexuar, Comares* and *Lions*); *Partal Palace* and *Yusuf III Palace*, in the Partal area; the *Abencerraje Palace* in the Secano area; and an important palace given to the Franciscans by the Catholic Monarchs so that they could establish a monastery there, which is today the location of the San Francisco Parador hotel. This is where the Catholic Monarchs were buried when it was a Franciscan monastery until they were later transferred to the Royal Chapel.

There were two well differentiated sectors in the complex: "upper Alhambra" in the south-east sector and "lower Alhambra" in the north-west, linked by two streets or main arteries: the *Calle Real Alta*[1] and the *Calle Real Baja*[2]. The Main Mosque was in the centre, since, as in all Muslims cities, it was the axis around which the city's activity rotated.

There were also three areas or quarters based on the activity or social strata of the people living there. The area where the people lived was called the *medina* (city). It was located in the place we now call the "Secano", in upper Alhambra. This was where officials, craftsmen, traders and other inhabitants who covered the main requirements of the city lived. The area where the garrison lived was the *military* quarter in the Alcazaba. Nobility and the upper class lived in the *residential* quarter, which, besides the Palaces or Royal Residence, covered the Partal area and the towers right up to the Generalife in lower Alhambra.

[1] The *Calle Real Alta* (Upper Royal Street) started at the now disappeared "Puerta Real" (Royal Gate), next to the Puerta del Vino (Gate of Wine) and went through the southern part of the Palace of Charles V along the current Calle Real and along the avenue that runs through the Secano until it came to the Torre del Cabo de la Carrera (Tower of the End of the Street).

[2] The *Calle Real Baja* (Lower Royal Street) ran parallel to the Calle Real Alta. It started from a square that has disappeared, Plaza de Comares, next to Comares Palace, and went along the southern facades of the palaces of Comares and the Lions, crossing the Partal until it came to the Tower of the Points where it ended.

Map documentation:

– Contreras, Rafael. *Estudio descriptivo de los monumentos árabes de Granada, Sevilla y Córdoba - 1878.*
– Pareja Bermúdez, Jesús. *El Partal y la Alhambra Alta.*
  (Notebook of the Caja de Ahorros, no. 46 - 1977).
– Díaz, Mari Luz (co-ordinator). *El espacio, la luz y las formas... aprendamos a ver la Alhambra.* Map on page 9.
  (Notebooks from the educational programme of the Patronato de la Alhambra y el Generalife – 2001).

THE CLIMB TO THE
Alhambra

The climb up to the monument is a lovely avenue running through the woods of the Alhambra, which is best done on foot to truly appreciate the beauty of the monument and the landscape.

There are several possible ways of reaching the Nasrid monument from the city. Due to its landscape and historic interest, the route followed in this book is the one that goes from Plaza Nueva, in the heart of the city, up to the monument through the woods of the Alhambra.

If you start off from this singular Granadine square and climb up the *Cuesta Gomérez* you will come to the beautiful

Puerta de las Granadas (Gate of Pomegranates), a Renaissance gate built by order of Emperor Charles V and designed by the artist Pedro Machuca around 1536, in the same rusticated style as the lower part of the Palace of Charles V inside the Alhambra.

The gate has three access arches. The one in the centre, which is the arch of triumph, is much larger than the side

ones. Above this main arch there is a fronton with the imperial coat of arms in the centre and three open pomegranates, which are the symbol of the city and lend their name to the gate, on the top. The pomegranate in the middle is held by two small sculptures representing angels lying down, according to Gómez Moreno,

or the figures of peace and abundance, according to Gallego and Burín.

Each arch leads to one of three paths: the one on the right takes us to Mauror hill, where the **Torres Bermejas** (Red Towers) are. They got this name from the colour of their walls, which date from the 8th century, and which were later reconstructed by al-Ahmar. Under these towers is the "Mauror" district, which was the Jewish quarter. The asphalted path in the middle winds its way after several bends to the complex of monuments of the Alhambra. The one on the left, called the "Cuesta de la Cruz" (Slope of the Cross), also leads to the Nasrid monument, and it is this latter one that will be followed here because of the beauty and artistic richness it has in store for us at the end, all surrounded by the Woods of the Alhambra, a marvellous spot first planted in the Christian age. The walkways are bordered by water streams which flow all year round. The water comes from the irrigation channels located above the Generalife, which flows into the River Darro.

In Arab times there were no woods, but there was a cemetery where al-Ahmar and his descendants were buried. The many poplar, chestnut and nettle trees, as well as other species, date from the 16th century and later reforestations in the 19th century.

The *Cuesta de la Cruz* we recommend you go along to reach the monument was created in 1599 by Leandro de Palencia. Besides being the shortest route, it ends up in a small square where the **Pilar de Carlos V** (Fountain of Charles V) and the **Puerta de Justicia** (Gate of Justice) are located. After you go through this gate you will come to the **Puerta del Vino** (Gate of Wine) after climbing for only a few metres.

THE FOUNTAIN OF CHARLES V

This is a lovely Renaissance monument designed by Pedro Machuca and built by the Italian Nicolao da Corte in 1545. It has three large stone masks spouting water out of their mouths, representing Granada's three rivers: *Darro, Genil* and *Beiro*. Above them is a cartouche in Latin referring to Emperor Charles V and right at the top is the imperial coat of arms. It also has other decorative motifs, such as some infants pouring water with conches and mythological scenes.

THE GATE OF JUSTICE

It was built in 1348 by Yusuf I. Carved onto the main front gate, which is shaped like a horseshoe, and exactly in the centre, is a hand with the open palm held out towards us, representing the five fundamental pillars of Islam: *unity of God, prayer, fasting or "ramadan", almsgiving and pilgrimage to Mecca.* Carved above the second arch is a key with a tassel, which may mean: the key to enter the "Medina" (city), or a symbol for the Granadine Nasrid sultans, as it is found in other rooms in the Alhambra, or the key to access paradise, related to following the five pillars of Islam described above. Three shells represent water, the Arab religious symbol par excellence. Above this gate, and in the centre of a band of original Persian mosaics of the age, is a niche with a statue of the Madonna and Child. This is a copy of the original, which is in the fine Arts Museum. The Catholic Monarchs ordered them to be placed there after the conquest of Granada in 1492 to symbolise the victory of Christianity over Islam.

Inside the gate there is a small winding passageway sloping upwards, an indication of its defensive purpose. The next facade is modest, with a horseshoe arch and some interesting remains of old enamelled clay tiles.

Top:
Fountain of Charles V.

Bottom:
Detail of one of the fountain's masks.

Next page:
Gate of Justice.

Right:
West facade of the Gate of Wine. The inhabitants of the Alhambra bought tax-free wine at this gate.

Top:
Detail of the east facade.

Bottom.
Detail of the west facade.

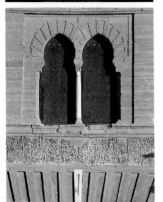

THE GATE OF WINE

Once you have gone through the *Gate of Justice*, you will come to a straight path which has a stretch of ramparts on the left, partly restored with marble slabs from the Arab cemetery ("Rauda") in the Alhambra. This path ends up in the **Plaza de los Aljibes** (Square of Cisterns) and the **Puerta del Vino** (Gate of Wine). The *Square* got its name from the underground water tanks the Count of Tendilla had built there. The *Gate* owes its name to the fact that wine was traded here, tax free, between the inhabitants of the Alhambra and merchants around the year 1556. It is obvious that the gate is not for military purposes, but rather the entrance to a street of the *medina* or city.

This gate has two facades dating from different times, with horseshoe arches. The *west* facade has a frieze of voussoirs, with the same key that is on the *Gate of Justice*. On the centre piece there is an inscription in plaster dating from Muhammad V's time and a small coupled window (double window). The *east* facade is very richly decorated with enamelled and glazed ceramics and above the frieze of voussoirs there is another coupled window, with plaster panels with plant motifs at the sides.

Decoration and ornamentation I:
Techniques, methods and decorative elements in Islamic architecture

Stuccoes in Lindaraja Mirador. Column capitals in the Courtyard of the Lions

Although many Islamic buildings seem to look simple and even modest on the outside, with hardly any motifs and decorative elements, inside they are usually profusely decorated, sometimes even from floor to ceiling, and not one empty space can be seen. This contrast between the outside and the inside is very evident in architecture found in the north of Africa and Spain. The reason is no other than the philosophy of life of the Muslim peoples, who lived their lives looking inwards, inside their homes and palaces.

It is curious to note that the decoration in some of the rooms in the Alhambra palaces is even more profuse than in other Muslim monuments, as the walls are totally covered and decorated from floor to ceiling with not a single space unadorned. An example of this is the *Salón de Embajadores* or *Salón del Trono* (Hall of Ambassadors or Throne Room) inside *Comares Tower*. This may well be an indication of a "fear of emptiness" (the Latin *horror vacui*), which *Johan Huizinga* referred to in his marvellous book[1] "The Autumn of the Middle Ages" as characteristic of the spirit's final periods. Perhaps the Granadine Nasrids already sensed that the *Arab-Andalusi* civilisation was in its final period, as indeed it was, when they built the Alhambra. The Alhambra could be seen as the Muslims' "swan song" in Al-Ándalus, since they were suffocated by increasing pressure from the Christian kingdoms and decided to leave a lasting testament in Granada.

As far as the techniques, methods and decorative elements of Islamic architecture are concerned, not as many decorative elements were used in Spanish Islamic architecture as in other places, perhaps as a result of the Peninsula's political and geographical isolation from the rest of the Islamic world. However, although there is not as much variety in the techniques and methods, the degree of virtuosity and perfection in completing them is exceptional.

[1] The book's author refers to Flemish painting in the 14th and 15th centuries in that case.

We will concentrate on the most important examples on the walls and ceilings of the rooms in the Alhambra.

STUCCO

This was probably the most widespread decorative method in the Islamic world as it was economical, easy to mould or carve and it could be adapted to all types of architectural surfaces: walls, columns, vaults, etc. Stucco enabled craftsmen to cover a poor and roughly finished surface and make it look rich, perfect and give it architectural virtuosity.

Stucco's basic component was gypsum plaster, normally mixed with other materials, such as marble or alabaster dust, giving it consistency and strength. First a mixture was prepared with water and these materials. When it was finished and had the right consistency, it was applied to the wall or surface to be covered, and it was then ready for decorative designs to be sculpted or moulded on it.

After the surface plastered with stucco had the required consistency, it was sculpted. This could be done directly, although normally the surface was drawn on first (for example with coal dust). A template with the decorative motif was used. It was placed on top of the wall or surface to be adorned, the template was covered with the coal dust, and when it was removed, the design was left on the surface. Now all the master craftsman had to do was patiently cut the drawn areas with the help of a small chisel.

This totally manual technique was slow and laborious. That is why, first in Persia and Iraq and then in Spain, the fast, precise "pouring" technique was used, which did not need as much labour. The difference was that the plaster mixture was put into wooden moulds containing the designs when it was still soft and taken out of the mould when it was dry.

The last process in both cases was the finish, which made the surface more consistent and bright and gave it more quality, with a patina with lime milk or other substances, depending on the final appearance required and on normal uses in each geographical area. In addition the finished surface was often painted with different colours, so that the background and the reliefs of the design were differentiated even further.

Detail of the walls in the Hall of Ambassadors. Stucco network, woven between the columns in the Courtyard of the Lions.

Example of the interplay of shapes and light produced by muqarna patterns.

"The Alhambra is like a carved plaster palace, where stucco is not only used to cover the walls but it even replaces them. A clear example of this is the *Patio de los Leones* (Courtyard of the Lions), where the function of the one hundred and thirty odd columns surrounding it is not to receive the loads conveyed by the fall of the arches, but to support the fine networks of carved stucco running from one to the other" (Dominique Clévenot and Gérard Degeorge, *Ornamentación del Islam*, p. 88).

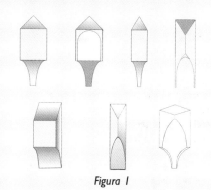

Figura I

MUQARNA

Arab muqarna are prisms or polyhedrons, normally made of wood or stucco, cut concavely at the bottom. The great peculiarity of geometrical designs based on muqarna is that any kind of surface or inverted volume can be covered with it, so it can be used to decorate ceilings, corbels, arches, pendentives, etc., although it is at its most surprising when it is used to decorate ceilings, such as those in the *Sala de Dos Hermanas* (Hall of the Two Sisters) and *Abencerrajes*, a true marvel in this decorative speciality.

Although these forms are also applied to wood, the most usual, as is the case in the Alhambra, is that they are made of stucco (plaster). Wooden moulds are used to make them. The craftsmen started the work from the bottom, positioning the wooden moulds, which were filled with plaster mixture. Once they were dry, they were taken out of the mould and they were carved and polished, giving them the final finish. There are seven basic prismatic shapes (figure I), which can be grouped in multiple, extremely ostentatious and complicated

combinations. These muqarna ceilings are a mathematical wonder, since the entire area is filled on the basis of combinations of geometrical forms and there are no empty spaces at all. The vaults of these ceilings usually finish in an octagonal star. Muqarna ceilings are an allegory of the stalactites in the cave where, according to Islamic tradition, the prophet Mahoma sheltered from his enemies in his flight from Mecca to Medina. They may also symbolise heaven or a bees' honeycomb.

Other different uses of muqarna can be found in the Alhambra, for example, on the pendentives or squinches that sometimes support the wooden ceilings, as in the *Sala de la Barca* (Boat Room), or in the pediment arches of some rooms, such as the *Sala de los Reyes* (Hall of the Kings) or at the entrance of the *Sala de la Barca*.

Detail of the ceiling of the hall linking Mexuar Courtyard with the Courtyard of the Myrtles.

WOOD

Another of the techniques in which Muslims were real masters was carpentry applied to architecture. Eaves of roofs, latticework, doors and windows... But the most noteworthy and surprising use of wood as a decorative element is in the ceilings. These were usually made of cedar because it was very ductile and resistant, as it is not attacked by the terrible woodworm. This work was basically done in one of two ways: either carving and sculpting the wood with geometrical designs or bows, or with marquetry inlay techniques, which consisted of creating designs on the wood by inlaying smaller pieces of other types of wood, such as ebony, lemon tree, sycamore, dyed wood, other materials, such as shell, bone, ivory, mother-of-pearl, silver or other fine metals. The final effect is a surprising interplay of shapes, colours and textures. There are numerous examples in the Alhambra, some of them reproductions of the original ceilings of former times. Perhaps the most important of them all is the one in the *Salón de Emba-jadores* (Hall of Ambassadors).

CERAMICS (*AZULEJOS* AND *ALICATADOS*)

When talking about ceramics in the context of decorating buildings, the Spanish refer to either *azulejos* or *alicatados*. They are similar concepts, although each word has a different etymology: "azulejo" comes from the Arabic word az-zulayan, which means glazed brick. "Alicatado" comes from the word al-qata'a, which

means a cut tile. "Alicatar" means to cover a surface with pieces of cut *azulejos*.

The technique of using ceramic tiles to decorate buildings appeared between the 11th and 12th centuries and was a revolution, even though the colours were not as varied at the beginning. The majority of them were different tones of blue. The *azulejo* tiles progressively became more and more important and the variety of colours also increased, above all in countries in the north of Africa and Spain, where this type of decorative technique became a real speciality, with a surprisingly high standard of finishes and geometrical perfection. It usually covers the bottom part of the wall and it is combined with stucco, which decorates the top part.

This decorative technique involves a long process, ranging from the **manufacture** of the tiles to **positioning** them on the wall. The first step of the manufacturing process is *making the paste* by mixing clay with water using rollers to obtain a wet, plastic mixture. Another stage is the *moulding* of the standard tiles required for a specific design. This moulding can be done either when the tile is still soft, before being fired, putting the mixture into moulds that shape it, or cutting the tile when it is dry and fired. The tiles are dried and fired in the kiln or muffle furnace. After firing and before glazing, the tile is called biscuit. The last step is *glazing* and *colouring*. The colours are obtained with the oxides of different metals: blue (cobalt), sapphire (copper dioxide), green (copper or chrome oxide)... Every colour needs a specific firing, dictated by the shine or finish required, so the tiles are put back into the furnace. The symbology certain colours have for Muslims is also very interesting: green is the Prophet's colour. Curiously all Muslim countries have this colour in their flag, especially Saudi Arabia's, the birthplace of Mahoma and Islam, which is completely green. Yellow is the colour of the sun, blue is the colour of the sky, Paradise. Red is the colour of blood, and warrior or erotic passion.

As far as positioning the tiles and their arrangement is concerned, this was not done directly onto the wall. After the tiles' outline had been established, either by cutting or by using moulds, they were filed so that they fitted perfectly into the design they would form part of. When the tiles were cut with a ruler and hit with a chisel or an "adze", many of them broke, which made the process quite expensive. That is why they were generally used with iron moulds, which shaped the tile when it was still soft. The small *azulejos* were assembled one by one, face down on the floor or on a plate. When all the tiles were in the correct place, they were covered with a mortar mixture. When this dried, the *azulejos* formed one flat block that was placed on the wall. The complicated nature of some of the designs and the small size of the tiles meant that

the craftsman putting it all together had to be very skilled. When the surface to be covered was curved rather than flat, it was even more difficult. In that case, the *azulejos* were assembled on concave surfaces with the shape of the wall or vault to be covered rather than on the floor or on a plate, and once the mortar mixture holding them together had dried, it was raised and fixed. The complexity also varied depending on the design, size and variety of the tiles forming it, as well as the arrangement they were placed in. In this respect, it could be said that there are two types of *azulejo* surrounds: some of them (photograph B), with a design formed by two, three or four different tiles, ranging in size from medium to large, prefabricated and moulded before being placed next to each other in a pattern where each one of the geometrical parts making up the whole (squares, triangles, stars...) can be easily distinguished, such as the surrounds in the *Patio de los Arrayanes* (Courtyard of the Myrtles). The second (photograph A), without a doubt much more complex to make, has a design formed by a multitude of different smaller pieces, the majority of them cut, which intertwine with each other forming networks and an interconnection of geometrical patterns, where it is more difficult to isolate each one of the pieces in the whole, such as those on the walls of the *Salón de Embajadores* (Hall of Ambassadors) or the *Sala del Mexuar* (Mexuar Hall).

Photograph A

Photograph B

The Alcazaba

This was the first of all the constructions in the Alhambra, and all the others were built in the shelter of the Alcazaba and the ramparts.

Left:
The Albaycin from the ramparts of the Alcazaba.

Right:
The Watch Tower, the highest of all the towers in the Alcazaba.

Bottom:
The Alcazaba seen from the Albaycin.

When al-Ahmar succeeded to the throne of Granada in 1238 he decided not to locate his palace in the *Old Alcazaba* or *Alcazaba Cadima* on the hill of the Albaycin, which had been the residence of the kings of Granada up until that time. Instead he chose to build it on Sabika hill, on the remains of a former castle which had stood there. As far as al-Ahmar was concerned, it was much safer to establish the defences and the palatine city on this hill, outside the enclosure of Granada, where there were no buildings and which provided easy access to the mountains and the sea. The Alcazaba was therefore the first of the Alhambra's constructions and the others built in the complex were protected by the Alcazaba and the ramparts.

It was built on bare rock, since the slopes were originally treeless. The woods surrounding it today date from the Christian period. It rises two hundred metres above the city of Granada and is triangular in shape, since this is easier to defend than a square or circular castle in the event of an attack. This fact, coupled with the height of its towers –the highest stand over twenty metres tall– made it an impregnable stronghold. It was never taken, as the surrender of Granada took place outside the Alhambra. The

Catholic Monarchs surrounded Granada, but the Christians never entered the Alhambra until after the surrender. Initially, part of it must have been equipped as al-Ahmar's residence, so it had a dual purpose at the beginning: alcazar (palace) and fortress. Later it was only used as a fortress.

Like the majority of the Alhambra, it has double ramparts, outside and inside. Between them there is a fosse or barbican, which was used as an internal path, and which would be filled with water in the event of an attack. The parapet walk at the top of the ramparts connected some towers with others. The Christians made some modifications later to the original fortress, such as "El Cubo" (The Cube), built on top of the Torre de la Tahona (Flourmill Tower) or the Jardín de los Adarves (Parapet Garden).

THE MILITARY QUARTER

Known in Spanish as the *Barrio Castrense*, this quarter took up the centre of the Alcazaba. Nowadays it is merely some ruins, but in Muslim times this was the location of the garrison's houses, where the soldiers who protected the Alhambra lived. You can see the typical layout of a Muslim house in these ruins: entrance, small courtyard with rooms off it (between two and four) and a latrine.

Top:
The military quarter. The Keep and Broken Tower are in the background.

Bottom:
The Keep from the military quarter.

One house stands out from all the others as it is much larger, almost three times as big as the rest, and it has a pool in the centre. It must have been the house of the head of the garrison.

THE ALCAZABA'S TOWERS

The most emblematic of all the towers is the *Torre de la Vela* (Watch Tower) which is also the tallest at a height of twenty-seven metres. Its name in Spanish comes from vigil or vigilance, since you could see everything that was happening in the surroundings from here. It was fitted with a bell in Christian times, which was used to regulate the irrigation of the Vega (fertile plain), as well as warn of earthquakes or fires and to sound the alarm. From this tower you can gaze at the wonderful scenery of the Albaycin, Granada, the Vega and the Sierra Nevada, so if possible, you should climb up to the top.

The *Torre de las Armas* (Tower of Weapons), housing the *Puerta de las Armas* (Gate of Weapons) is on the north side. It was the main access to the Alcazaba, which was used by people coming from the Albaycin after crossing the Cadí Bridge over the River Darro to enter the stronghold and go up to the Alhambra. It is a military style gate with a pronounced slope and winding access. It owes its name to the fact that on entering the citadel, people had to leave their weapons here and then pick them up again when leaving. The stables are next to it.

The *Torre del Homenaje* (Keep) is at the north-west apex and next to it, on the east side, is the *Torre de la Quebrada* (Broken Tower). Both of them are twenty-two metres high and the most moderate in decoration. Below them are the dungeons. The third tower on this west side is the *Torre del Adarguero*

Top left:
The fosse of the Alcazaba. The Watch Tower is in the background.

Top right:
The Keep and lower ramparts. The fosse and parapet walk can also be seen.

Bottom:
Gate of Weapons.

(Tower of the Leather Shield Bearer) which is much lower, but which may have originally been as high as the other two before it on this side. In the south, and in what has been the Parapet Garden since Christian times, are the *Torre de la Pólvora* (Powder Tower) and *Torre de la Sultana* (Tower of the Sultana).

THE PARAPET GARDEN

This beautiful garden, known as the *Jardín de los Adarves* in Spanish, located in the south of the Alcazaba, takes its name from the Spanish word "adarve", which means parapet, the top part of the ramparts where the parapet walk is. The fosse of this part of the Alcazaba was filled with earth and transformed into a Garden by the Marquis of Mondéjar in the 17th century. In the corner of the garden where the *Powder Tower* is located, there is a small balcony from where you can see the city, the Sierra Nevada, the Torres Bermejas (Red Towers) and the Vega. And on a wall, carved into stone, you can read the famous poem written by Francisco de Icaza when he saw a blind man playing his guitar and waiting for some money: *"Dale limosna mujer, que no hay en la vida nada, como la pena de ser ciego en Granada"* (Give him alms, lady, for there is no greater misery in life than being blind in Granada).

Top:
Parapet Garden and Tower of the Sultana.

Bottom:
Powder Tower in the Parapet Garden.

Decoration and ornamentation II:
Most frequent subjects and decorative motifs

If there is something that characterises the decoration of Islamic buildings it is the fact that there is a series of shared and almost constant subjects or decorative motifs, which are repeated uniformly regardless of the technique or decorative material used. There are three of these large decorative motifs: calligraphy, plants and geometrical designs.

CALLIGRAPHIC MOTIFS

Although other cultures did not use calligraphy in their decorative art, apart from the codices of Christianity and more isolated examples, it became an extremely important decorative motif in the Islamic civilisation. Calligraphy in Islamic buildings not only fulfils a decorative function, but also an iconographic one, comparable to and substituting the function images have in the Christian world. It serves

to preserve and manifest the word of God. It is used to structure surfaces, for example, separating, as a strip, the join between the *alicatado* (tiled) surround of a wall from the top part, covered with stucco, or to frame a window, or the curve of an arch or a doorway.

There are two types of calligraphy:

-Kufic: this script, characterised by its rectilinear and angular appearance, comes from the city of Kufa in Iraq and it is the one that first appeared in architectural ornamentation. It is an educated script that only the learned and the imams (priests) knew how to read. In the Alhambra it is found on the *azulejos* in the *Salón de Embajadores* (Hall of Ambassadors).

-Cursive: there is an example of this script on this page. It appears in architectural ornamentation from the 12th century. It is a script that is connected, almost circular and flexible, which was only used in official and administrative writings in the beginning, but which ended up becoming widespread and used in architectural ornamentation, as it was the script that the majority of the people knew (or rather the majority of the people who knew how to read and write, since a large part of the population was illiterate). Almost all the inscriptions in the Alhambra are cursive.

Most of the contents of the calligraphy decorating the walls of the buildings are passages from the Koran. The entire Alhambra is filled with religious writings, such as the leitmotif "ONLY ALLAH IS VICTORIOUS", which is repeated ad infinitum. Poetry is also often found in the Alhambra, despite the fact that this was extremely rare in Islam before the 14th century. The poetry sings the praises of the palace and its sultans or it contains symbolical allegories. The two most famous poets of the Nasrid monument are Ibn Zamrak, the most important, and Ibn Yayyab.

PLANT MOTIFS

Although pre-existing arts had already made use of plant ornamentation, it changed from being a secondary motif to having the central and most prominent place in Islamic decorative arts, adorning large surfaces and even entire walls. This focus on everything that represents nature can be explained by their religious faith, the constant references made in the Koran to Paradise, understood to be a "Garden of Happiness".

Plant ornamentation could be classified into two large groups. The first would contain elements that could be classed as "a more simple naturalism", flowers, plants, trees, pineapples, shells...The walls of the Alhambra are full of this type of motifs, such as on the pediment arch leading to the *Sala de la Barca* (Boat Room), where five trees are engraved on either side of the arch, including their trunks, different leaves and fruits, representing the Garden of Eden. Another element that appears many times, and perhaps the most important, is shells, symbolising water, blessing and the word of Allah. They are found everywhere. However, their symbology is greater in the oratories, such as those in *Mexuar* and *Partal*, where they always appear in threes, crowning the Mihrab.

The other type of plant ornament is *arabesque*, which could be classified as "abstract naturalism". The plant forms are denaturalised, becoming a repetitive and geometrical motif. Arabesque is a "geometrical" pattern, whose main element is a stem extending in a continuous line, turning in different directions, with no limits to its growth, along the entire surface of the design. A series of secondary leafy stems arise from that stem, covered in leaves, canes or bunches, filling the empty spaces. The symmetry and harmony with which arabesque covers spaces is based on the same mathematical principles governing pure geometrical decoration. Sometimes this type of pattern becomes so abstract that the main stem no longer exists, consisting instead of leaves or motifs that appear to be vegetation-based overlapping each other, thus taking over all the space in a dynamic and rhythmical manner. Arabesque is one of the most frequent motifs in the stucco decorating the walls of the Alhambra.

GEOMETRICAL MOTIFS

Muslims inherited the use of geometrical motifs to decorate buildings from classic architecture, but they perfected them and gave them a level of complexity and development that had been previously unknown, turning geometrical decoration into a first-class art form. Although geometrical motifs appear in all the materials used in architectural ornamentation (stucco, wood, brick,...), they have the most impact when used in the covering of walls with ceramic tiles (*azulejos* or *alicatados*).

Geometrical regularities based on figures that repeat, colours that follow a standard pattern and geometrical transformations, such as

Arabesque details with alternating pineapples and shells in the Courtyard of the Lions and the Mihrab in the Partal Oratory.

symmetries, rotations and translations, are all to be found in the decorative motifs adorning the *alicatados* in the Alhambra. The geometry in the ornamentation can be perceived in very different ways, depending on how we look at the arrangement of the figures, and the repetition of the motifs stretches space out infinitely in all directions. This is an invitation to look at the same *alicatado* again and again and to be surprised with new images every time. The symmetry of the shapes can be perceived as order and harmony. Well-organised colour and geometry fire our imagination and the enjoyment of aesthetics. Underlying these techniques there is always a response to a classic problem in geometry: which geometrical figures can cover a surface, positioning them next to each other, without leaving gaps or overlapping them? Let's analyse some of the most representative patterns in the Alhambra.

Figure 1: sketch of the bow tie pattern

One of the most representative formations, known as the "bow tie" is found, among other places, in some of the surrounds in the *Patio de los Arrayanes* (Courtyard of the Myrtles). The space is structured by means of equilateral triangles that are exactly the same. A triangle is always the starting point. It is then modified by cutting three circular segments from it. These segments are then repositioned to maintain the surface of the original triangle. That is how this well-known "bow tie" obtains its final shape. A six-pointed star and a hexagon, placed alternately in the centre, complete the formation. Figure 1 shows the graphic sketch of the final pattern as a whole. The photograph of this motif appears on page 33.

Another of the shapes appearing most often is the star, whose infinite combinations (with 8, 16 or more points) come from rotating squares. Let's take an 8-pointed star as an example. It is produced by rotating a square with an angle of 45° (figure 2A). The complex network of small squares each large square is divided up into serves as a guide to trace the figures forming the star and the links in the design (figure 2B). The final composition, shown in the photograph accompanying the figures, can combine stars with a different number of points that have been assembled together to form a network, in which the link is the decorative motif joining and running through the design. The final impression is a type of never-ending maze formed of multiple coloured shapes, which, seen as a whole, give us another perspective of the geometrical landscape.

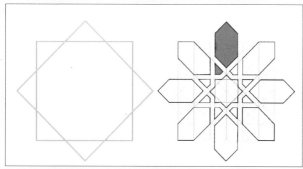

Figure 2A   Figure 2B

THE NASRID
Palaces

They form the Royal Residence,
or Alcazar, where the official and
family life of the Nasrid kings took
place. They are a complex
of three palaces,
built independently, and each one
has a different purpose.

They form the Royal Residence, or Alcazar, where the official and family life of the Nasrid kings took place. They are on one side of the complex of monuments rather than right in the centre and they face the Albaycin. They are actually a complex of three palaces which were built over an extended period rather than at the same time. **The Mexuar** was the first and so at the beginning it was both the monarch's official residence and family dwelling place. Later, during the time of Yusuf I, **Comares Palace** was built and lastly, Muhammad V had the **Palace of the Lions** built. Each one of these palaces, built independently, coexisted as three very well differentiated quarters and areas and each had its own purpose. The *Mexuar* was used as an area for audiences with the public and the administration of justice. *Comares Palace* was the king's official residence and the *Palace of the Lions*, identified as the "harem", was the royal family's private dwelling place, which only those closest to them could access. These three independent palaces were later joined together, after the taking of Granada, and they were all used as a single palace.

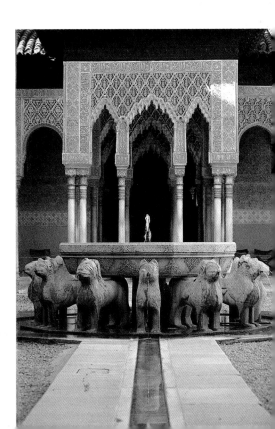

Nasrid PALACES

Nasrid
PALACES

MEXUAR PALACE

1. Machuca Garden
2. Machuca Tower
3. Mexuar Hall
4. Oratory
5. Mexuar Courtyard
6. Golden Room
7. Facade of Comares Room

COMARES PALACE

8. Courtyard of the Myrtles
9. South Gallery
10. North Gallery (hidden by the perspective of the drawing)
11. Boat Room (hidden by the perspective of the drawing)
12. Hall of Ambassadors (hidden, it continues on from the Boat Room, occupying the space of Comares Tower)
13. Comares Tower

PALACE OF THE LIONS

14. Courtyard of the Lions
15. Muqarna Hall
16. Harem Courtyard
17. Hall of the Abencerrajes
18. Hall of the Kings
19. Hall of the Two Sisters
20. Lindaraja Mirador

ROYAL BATHS

21. Vaulted ceilings of some rooms in the Baths

CHRISTIAN SECTION IN THE NASRID PALACES

22. Emperor's Rooms
23. Courtyard of the Railings or the Cypresses
24. Lindaraja Courtyard
25. Queen's Boudoir
26. Overhead passageway connecting the Hall of Ambassadors with the Emperor's Rooms

PARTAL GARDENS

1. Partal Palace or Tower of the Ladies
2. Partal Pond
3. Arab houses in the Partal
4. Oratory
5. Gardens
6. Remains of the Palace of Yusuf III (located at the edge of the drawing)

PARTAL GARDENS AND THE PALACE OF CHARLES V

Entrance to
the palaces

═══ PALACE OF CHARLES V

1. West facade (entrance)
2. Alhambra Museum (mezzanine floor)
3. Courtyard

4. Fine Arts Museum (top floor)
5. Chapel
6. Introductory room

DIBUJO: MESAMADERO

The Mexuar

This is the oldest of the three palaces forming the Royal Residence. On certain days it was used as the hall of Audience, Justice and Advice for the citizens of Granada. The different parts in it are: *Jardín de Machuca* (Machuca Garden), *Sala del Mexuar* (Mexuar Hall) and *Patio del Mexuar* (Mexuar Courtyard).

MACHUCA GARDEN

It is on the east side and it has an arched gallery with a tower next to it and a garden with a geometrical design with a lovely pool in the middle. It must originally have had another gallery opposite the one still standing. It owes its name to the fact that Machuca, the architect of the Palace of Charles V, lived in this garden's tower and rooms. This was where the original entrance to the palace was for those who came from the Almanzora district and the Albaycin.

MEXUAR HALL

The hall preserved today is a far cry from the original, as it was altered by the Christian kings. In Arab times, the ceiling was open in the centre, letting the only light come in through a lantern. There was a raised chamber, closed by latticework, where the sultan would sit to listen to his citizens' requests, without being seen. The side windows did not exist. When Charles V and the Christian Monarchs adopted it as a chapel, the following alterations were made: the lantern in the ceiling was closed, the side windows were opened up, an altar was placed against the entrance wall, flanked by ceramic panels, which depict Hercules' columns with the motto "Plus Ultra"; the raised chamber where the sultan sat was removed and in its place the chapel choir stall was built, of which only the front remains. The rest of the hall's decoration

Left:
Exterior view of Mexuar Palace.

Top:
Detail of Machuca Courtyard.

Bottom:
Detail of Comares facade in Mexuar Courtyard.

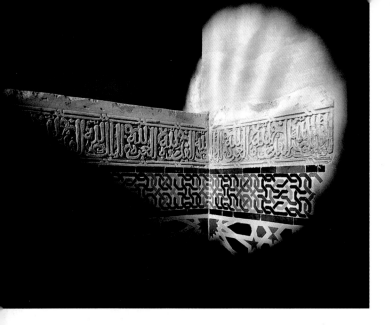

Top:
Detail of the walls in Mexuar Hall.

Right:
Mexuar Hall, which has changed considerably from its original state as a result of Christian alterations. At the back, and better lit, is the Oratory.

is original of the age with some retouching. You can see *Machuca Garden* from the windows.

At the back of this hall is **the Oratory**, a small room from where the Albaycin can be seen, with the remains of the ramparts surrounding it. The top part of the room is decorated with the frieze "Only God is victorious" and the Nasrid coat of arms. There is a niche, or "Mihrab", the equivalent to our altar, at one end of the oratory, where only the priest or "Iman" could enter to lead the prayers. It is east-facing, looking towards the sacred city of Mecca, the place where Muslims have to pray towards in prostration.

MEXUAR COURTYARD

The *Patio del Mexuar* is located at the exit of the Sala del Mexuar (Mexuar Hall). As it is not large, with a small marble basin in the centre, it is easy to see that its purpose was to provide separation and access. It has two facades: the *north* one, a portico with three arches leading to the *Cuarto Dorado* (Golden Room), and the *south* one, the *facade of the Cuarto de Comares* (Comares Room).

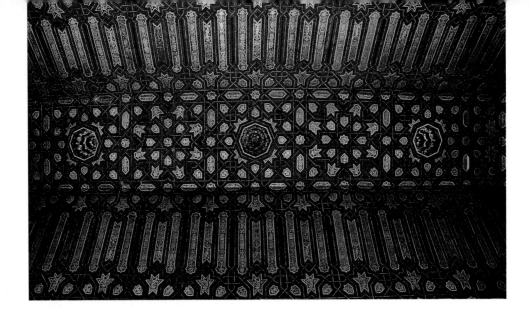

The **Golden Room** is a small chamber with a wooden ceiling decorated with Arab work, which was gilded with "gold leaf" in the Christian age. This room was used in Arab times for the meetings of the Court of Justice and as a reception room for ambassadors, so it served as a link between the public palace (*Mexuar*) and the official palace ("*Diwan*" or *Comares Palace*).

The Facade of Comares Room is splendid as a result of its rich decoration and design. At the top there are wooden eaves made of cedar with decorative motifs of pineapples and shells. Below it are windows closed with wooden latticework belonging to the rooms of the concubines, who would look through them without being seen. The two doors, which are rectangular and not horseshoe arches, edged with a ceramic frieze, mark the entrance to the sultan's official residence.

By going through the door on the left, and following a stepped and right-angled route, you come to the *Diwan* or *Comares Palace*. It is worth noting that the entrance to a Muslim house, stronghold or palace is never in a straight line, so that visitors are disconcerted and getting in and out are more difficult and they are therefore at the mercy of their host. The soldiers guarding the entrance would sit on the marble benches on either side of it.

Top:
Ceiling in the Golden Room. It was gilded with "gold leaf" in Christian times.

Left:
Mexuar Courtyard and facade of the Golden Room.

Next page:
Mexuar Courtyard and facade of Comares Palace.

Comares Palace (Diwan)

This palace was built by Yusuf I. It is thought that its use changed after the Palace of the Lions, the third one, was built. When it coexisted with the latter palace, it was used as the king's workplace, where the court's official life took place. Its most significant rooms are: *Patio de los Arrayanes* (Courtyard of the Myrtles), the *Sala de la Barca* (Boat Room) and the *Salón de Embajadores* (Hall of Ambassadors).

THE COURTYARD OF THE MYRTLES

This rectangular courtyard is the centre of the palace and its purest lines of Arab architecture measure thirty-seven metres long by almost twenty-four metres wide. The water behaves like a marvellous mirror here where everything takes on a double dimension. Everything is reflected in the pool with millimetric precision, giving us the sensation of eternity. The two circular fountains at the ends represent the vital process: the jet is

Top left:
Detail of one of the niches at the entrance to the Boat Room.

Top right:
Latticework and fretwork in the Courtyard of the Myrtles.

Next page:
Courtyard of the Myrtles from the Boat Room. On the floor, one of the circular fountains in the courtyard symbolising the cycle of life.

birth, which when it falls forms a pool in a wide circle, which is the continuation of life. It then runs through a narrow channel, which are the twilight years, to end up pouring into the large central pond, eternity. Two rows of myrtles, planted on both sides of the water, are the reason for the courtyard's name.

The two galleries on the north and south sides are the same, with seven semicircular arches with slender muqarna capitals. There are two openings on both sides, which were used as a meeting place for the king's visitors and his secretaries, ministers,

etc. They would talk in these alcoves before the official audience, drinking tea and smoking the water pipe. The *south gallery* is adjacent to the Palace of Charles V, with which it is linked through its crypt. The *north gallery*, crowned by Comares Tower, connects the courtyard with the Boat Room and the Hall of Ambassadors. On the walls are poems by Ibn Zamrak, who was a notable poet and also a minister of Muhammad V.

BOAT ROOM

The *Sala de la Barca* is located in the north gallery of the courtyard. It is entered through a pointed arch with beautiful plant motifs on its spandrels. There are two richly carved marble niches in the reveals of this arch with coloured tiles inside. They were used for standing vases of water with flowers or oil lamps, depending on whether it was day or night.

This room was the anteroom of the royal hall (*Hall of Ambassadors*). Its name either comes from the shape of its ceiling, an inverted boat, or the transcription of the Arabic word "baraka", which means blessing, on the interior frieze. The ceiling is made in the classic inlay or marquetry style, which the Arabs started in Spain. However, it is not original, since a large part of it was burned in

Top:
General view of the Courtyard of the Myrtles.
The north gallery and Comares Tower
are in the background.

the 1890 fire. It seems that this room was used as the sultans' throne room.

HALL OF AMBASSADORS

The *Salón de Embajadores* is just behind the *Boat Room*. It is the largest and highest room in the entire palace. It was built in the shape of a perfect cube and located inside *Comares Tower*. There are openings in its sides for nine alcoves and windows that were closed by coloured glass called "cumarias" in Arabic, which is where the current name of the tower comes from.

The decoration looks like large stucco tapestries hanging on the wall and there are different models: shells, flowers, stars... This gives us an idea of the naturalist style of Arab architecture, which tries to bring nature into the home, by showing the real natural world through large outdoor-facing windows, by means of interior gardens and courtyards, or in the perfect abstraction or symbolism represented in this stucco work, tiles and ceilings. The reason for this love of naturalism lies in their pantheist mentality, of seeing God in the living expression of his creation. The relief part of the hall was totally gold polychromed and the deeper parts have different colours, but they are always light.

Another of the constants on the walls in this hall are the writings in the plasterwork. There are two types here, mentioned in the section on decoration and ornamentation (page 39): kufic and cursive. Kufic is an educated straight-lined script, which few people knew. It can be seen on the lower part of the wall, on the tiles. Cursive script is the normal one and the majority of the inscriptions in the Alhambra are of this type.

The lower part of the walls is decorated with *azulejo* tiles and the ones in this hall are possibly the most richly decorated in the entire palace. The mosaic decoration is centred around a star with eight points in the centre and other stars going around it forming concentric circles. The colours alternate in circles around the central one forming a geometric progression. As stated in the pages of this book on decoration and ornamentation, all Arab art is intimately related to spiritual and mathematical perfection, which they were masters of. Proof of this is their numeric system, which is the one we use today, and treatises on algebra, which they invented. The colours used most are yellow, blue, green and black.

The floor is not the original one, which deteriorated and was restored around 1815. The original was made of glazed white and blue ceramics. Only a small part of this type of mosaic remains in the centre of the hall.

The ceiling is a masterpiece of Muslim carpentry. The vault is eighteen metres high and it is made of cedar wood with inlays of different colours forming stars. There are seven crowns of concentric stars up to the small central cupola, which represents *Islamic Paradise*. Each crown is one of the seven heavens that have to be ascended to reach this *Paradise*. The four

Right:
Hall of Ambassadors from the Boat Room.

Top left:
Ceiling in the Hall of Ambassadors.
You can see the seven crowns of stars
preceding the central cupola, which
represents "Islamic Paradise".

Top right:
Detail of one of the Hall's alcoves.

Next page:
The interior of the Hall of Ambassadors.

diagonals of the ceiling are the four trees or the four rivers of that *Islamic Paradise,* which is a garden, or Eden, as in the Old Testament.

But what was the royal arrangement of the hall like? The "Royal Residence" needs to be understood as a home that was lived in, and not just a cold museum. Everything was thought out precisely and arranged accordingly. Nothing was left to chance. Everything had a reason, whether mystic, mathematical or esoteric. The cube-shaped room represents the world; the cupola, heaven; everything is under God. The king's viziers would sit in the alcoves or at the windows so that the king in the centre could dominate over the entire space of the hall and outside. Visitors or ambassadors who had an audience with him came from outside the courtyard, fully lit by the light of day. The king and his ministers were inside the hall surrounded by the faint light that filtered through the coloured glass in the windows. This meant that visitors were in an inferior position, as they were totally lit up by the brightness outside while the person they were talking to remained in the semidarkness.

A very important detail we need to know to understand Arab houses is the play of light and the large windows. The ones at the top are only for show and to let some air in. The light actually comes from the bottom part. The windows are low because Arabs reclined on

the floor on cushions and divans. The room was heated by braziers and lit by oil lamps. All of the Alhambra was made to be seen from the floor, which is the place where all the spaces and plays of light combine.

And finally, some history. This was the Hall where Boabdil met with his noblemen and agreed to surrender Granada. This is also the place where that surrender was signed and where Charles V, surprised by the beauty of this citadel and city, exclaimed: "Unhappy is he who has lost so much beauty".

The Palace of the Lions (harem)

The *Palacio de los Leones*, the third palace of the Royal Residence, was for the private use of the king and his family. The centre is taken up by the extremely well-known *Patio de los Leones* (Courtyard of the Lions), which is surrounded by other halls and rooms: *Sala de los Mocárabes* (Muqarna Hall), *Sala de Abencerrajes* (Hall of the Abencerrajes), *Sala de los Reyes* (Hall of the Kings) and *Sala de Dos Hermanas* (Hall of the Two Sisters). After these rooms, and following the itinerary of the visit, there are more quarters, some built by the Christians and some by the Arabs, such as *the baths*, which are extremely interesting.

The construction of the palace was started at the time of Muhammad V, the son of Yusuf I, in 1377 and the architect was Aben Cencid (or Cean), according to Rafael Contreras, the Alhambra's conservation architect. Although it is rather large for living quarters, there is little doubt that this was its purpose (harem) due to the layout of a group of alcoves around the courtyard, with a high open floor, no windows looking outside and the interior garden, characteristic of the "hortus

conclusus" (enclosed garden) which is in keeping with the Arab idea of paradise and also because the word harem "al haram" is an indication of sanctuary.

THE COURTYARD OF THE LIONS

Everything here is an allegory of paradise and the result is a real living and petrified oasis. The one hundred and twenty-four Macael marble

Previous page:
Courtyard of the Lions from Muqarna Hall.

Top:
Detail of one of the Courtyard's galleries.

Left:
Detail of the fountain.

columns (from Almeria) surrounding the courtyard symbolise a forest of palm trees. The columns have a lead sheet between the capital and the shaft, and another between the shaft and the base, which act as an expansion joint and seismic resisting system in the event of an earthquake.

There are doubts, however, about what was on the floor of the courtyard in Nasrid times. There is a theory that maintains that there was a garden planted here, which may have been at a lower level than the current floor, so that the flowers and shrubs would not obstruct the view of the courtyard as they grew, forming a kind of carpet of colours. This garden idea is supported not only by some old drawings, but also because it is referred to in some verses by Ibn Zamrak, which are on the surround in the Hall of the Two Sisters. Another more recent theory maintains that there were no plants and that the oldest descriptions of this courtyard state that it was paved with marble slabs and that the garden seen in some old engravings was planted after the Nasrid age.

The layout of the courtyard is not entirely true Arab style, as, to a certain extent, it is similar to a courtyard of a Roman house. And the cloister surrounding it is without a doubt Christian influence. Its design is extremely

complicated, as it has seven symmetry axes. The shape of the two small pavilions opposite each other on the east and west sides remind us of the typical nomad's tent of the Arab peoples.

Four streams flow from each one of the wings towards the centre where they disperse under the fountain. They are the four streams of paradise stemming from the rooms surrounding the garden, which are located on a higher level so that the water can flow down and therefore, as it is used for ablutions, always be clean.

The most striking element of the courtyard is the fountain, which is how it got its name. There

are countless legends about its origin and meaning. What does this fountain represent in the centre of the harem? Some people think it represents the twelve months of the year. Others say they are the twelve signs of the zodiac, others, more legendary, refer to the lions as the tears of a princess, which, when they fell onto the courtyard, emerged as twelve lions. However, the most likely, since the shape and number coincide, is the one that explains its origin in Hebrew art, in the "Sea of Bronze" of Solomon's temple. There are twelve white

Spain and which gave the country supremacy in the western world, above all in Cordoba, Toledo, Seville and finally in Granada. The basin on the lions, with verses by Ibn Zamrak, is Arab in origin, but it is not original, as there was another basin before it.

MUQARNA HALL

Of the four halls surrounding the courtyard, the *Sala de los Mocárabes* is the first one you come across when you enter from the *Patio de los Arrayanes* (Courtyard of the Myrtles). Its name may come from the three muqarna arches that lead onto the courtyard or from the vault covering it, which was made of muarna. Part of the current ceiling was placed in the 18th century. It is the least interesting of the four.

HALL OF THE ABENCERRAJES

The *Sala de Abencerrajes* is on the south side of the *Courtyard* and it was apparently the king's chamber. In the centre of this square room is the famous fountain where, according to the legend that lends its name to this hall, the thirty-six Abencerraje nobles were decapitated. All their throats were slit because the sultan's favourite committed adultery with one of these nobles. The king, helped by the declaration made by the Zegris against them, invited them to his room and as they walked in, he decapitated them, letting their blood fall into the basin so as not to alert the others. All this happened in

Top left:
Central fountain of the Courtyard of the Lions. Written on the basin it says that if the lions have no life, they cannot vent their fury.

Bottom right:
Detail of the columns and the muqarna next to Muqarna hall.

marble lions holding up the sea, the twelve lions of Judah or the twelve tribes of Israel. A factor favouring this theory is the fact that two of them are marked with an equilateral triangle on their foreheads, which represent the two chosen tribes (Judah and Levi). The fact that it dates from the 11th century, prior to the palace's construction, and that it was located in the house of the Jewish vizier and poet Samuel Ibn Negrela, who gave it to his king, means there are few doubts about the matter. It was a beautiful gift, which reminds us of the peace and coexistence of the three monotheist religions (Jewish, Muslim and Christian) in medieval times in

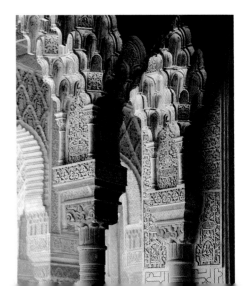

The plasterwork is mainly original, as are the colours. However, the surround along the lower part of the wall is not original, as it is Andalusian style and comes from the tile factory in Seville, dated around the 16th century.

The top part is taken up by the "Chanan", which was the upper harem or the harem of women. It has long continuous corridors with courtyards for relaxing in and balconies opening out onto the *Patio de los Leones* (Courtyard of the Lions).

the reigns of Muley Hacem, Boabdil or Muhammad XI "the Lame".

The entire panorama of the outside world is reflected above this fountain. The beautiful cupola rises up in the ceiling, shaped like an eight-pointed star, made of plaster muqarna, giving you the sensation of being in a stalactite cave, with its lake represented by the fountain.

As it was a private room, there are no windows looking outside, so that no-one could meddle in the king's private affairs. The latticework at the top is only for letting some light pass through. The room is divided into two equal parts on both sides, one for the bedroom and one for the living room and it would have been decorated only with low tables, couches, divan beds and braziers. The structure of an Arab house is not like a European one, with a large number of rooms to live in and an excess of unnecessary furniture.

HALL OF THE KINGS

The *Sala de los Reyes* is located in the east of the courtyard. It is the longest hall in the harem and it is divided into three equal rooms, with another two smaller rooms, which may have been cupboards judging by their location and lack of light. The rooms have vaults with Morisco paintings on leather, which portray scenes of frontier tales. The painting in the central section represents ten Moorish kings who may have been kings of the Alhambra, above all because two of them have red beards. One could be the king called "The Red". The almond shape of their eyes, their clothes, as well as their sword-belts and swords leave us in no doubt that the painter was a Morisco. The hall gets its name from the paintings in this central room. The paintings in the side rooms may have suffered from Christian influences, especially due to the subjects they contain: Christian knights and ladies. This may have been a result of the good relations between Muslims and Christians in the reigns of Muhammad V and Peter I "The Cruel". This Christian king even asked the Moorish king of Granada for help to restore his palaces in the Royal Alcazares of Seville. These paintings have been the subject of much debate, especially as they have human figures, which it seems Koranic laws prohibited, or at least they are not represented very often.

This hall, the longest in the entire harem, and even in the Royal Residence, covered with cupolas made of muqarnas, has a curious layout. It may have been the council or meeting room of the sultan and his ministers or generals, to deal with matters of state or justice and they may have entered through an isolated door, which is near the hall of the third small room. But it is difficult to imagine the sultan letting anyone come into this hall because it is part of the harem. It would not be at all unlikely for it to have been used for family occasions or in the summer, as it would have been much cooler, since the large open rooms in this hall have no doors. The first mass was said here when the Catholic Monarchs entered Granada.

Previous page:
Hall of the Kings.
This was where the first mass was held in the Alhambra when the Catholic Monarchs entered Granada.

Bottom:
Paintings on leather in one of the side rooms of the Hall of the Kings. They represent medieval scenes of Muslims and Christians.

HALL OF THE TWO SISTERS

The *Sala de Dos Hermanas* is located next to the *Hall of the Kings* on the north side of the courtyard, and it is one of the most beautiful in this palace. There are two theories to explain the origin of its name. The first maintains that it comes from the two central Macael white marble slabs on the floor on both sides of the central fountain. They are exactly the same size (the largest in the Alhambra), colour and weight. Another theory, perhaps more likely, refers to the poetry written on the walls in this hall. One of them could give us the origin of the name: "The constellation of Gemini holds out its hand to you in a sign of friendship and the moon goes up to it to talk in secret". So we have the twins (Gemini) approaching the hall.

The room was for distinguished ladies or the sultan's favourites, who had a certain amount of independence. It has a mirador looking out over the city and it connected directly with the baths through a small door on the left.

As in the *Hall of the Abencerrajes*, there are two small doors next to the entrance of this room. The one on the right leads to the "chanan" or upper harem. The other one on the left is the entrance to a toilet. However, there are no traces of kitchens in the entire harem. Arabs cooked on portable cookers or stoves, so the soot disappeared quickly and the smell of food did not linger. In the palace, cooking was done outside so as not to mix the odour with the scent of the flowers.

The hall's cupola is splendid and it is worth noting the openings made in it, giving you the sensation of distance and movement, again evoking the symbolism of the heavenly vault. At the back of the hall is the *Lindaraja Mirador*.

LINDARAJA MIRADOR

This small room was the place where the sultan's favourite relaxed. Its name comes from breaking down the Arabic words that form it: "Lin-dar-Aixa", in other words "Sultana's Residence". Due to its exquisiteness and beauty, it is one of the most spectacular rooms in the Alhambra. Attention was paid to every last detail in this room, since it must have been majestic as the day came to a close. It has a wonderful wooden cupola with coloured inlaid glass, which colours the walls when the sun shines through it. The room looked out onto Granada and the valley of the River Darro, perfect for daydreaming and resting. The windows are low, because this was required by the Muslim tradition of reclining on the floor on cushions and ottomans. The view of the city was lost when Emperor Charles V had a pavilion built next to the room, which completely surrounded the mirador. Unfortunately, to alleviate the misfortunate event, he had the garden planted, which is really a courtyard, just below the *Lindaraja Mirador*. It is known as the *Lindaraja Garden* or *Courtyard*.

After this area of the palace you come across rooms and chambers that are the result of new constructions and alterations of already existing ones, carried out by the Christians, which, together with the *Baths*, end the itinerary of the palaces.

Christian section in the Nasrid Palaces

When the Catholic Monarchs conquered Granada they were so surprised by how beautiful the Nasrid Palace was that they even made it their residence for when they visited Granada. They called it the "Royal Residence of the Alhambra". As already mentioned in these chapters, they also modified and repaired some of the quarters. When Charles V came to Granada, which coincided with his honeymoon after marrying Isabella of Portugal, he also knew how to appreciate the hospitality and beauty of the city and of such a singular monument. He then decided to build a new palace within the framework of the Royal Residence, but with a style more in tune with the western way of life and culture. It was to be known as the "New Royal Residence" to differentiate it from the previous one.

Nevertheless, as the construction of this new palace would be costly and take some time to complete, some rooms were built within the Arab palace, or Old Royal Residence, which no doubt cost far less and were built much faster than those in the future Palace of Charles V. These quarters were to be used by the Emperor and his family on their future visits to Granada.

These new rooms were an extension of the Royal Residence and they are at the end of the itinerary.

THE EMPEROR'S ROOMS

They are next to the *Hall of the Two Sisters*. The only room that can be visited is the living room. It is decorated with coffered ceilings and the motto "Plus Ultra" together with the initials "K" and "Y", representing the names of the Emperor and his Empress ("K" for Karl, or Karlo V and "Y" for Ysabel, his wife, the Princess of Portugal). Later,

Previous page:
Lindaraja Mirador.

Top left:
Detail of one of the paintings inside the Queen's Boudoir.

Top right:
Gallery built in Christian times. The Tower of the Queen's Boudoir is in the background.

the American writer Washington Irving used three of these rooms when he lived in the Alhambra. This is where he wrote the extremely famous *Tales of the Alhambra*, which have helped a great deal to spread the fame of the monument and Granada. A marble plaque in memory of this writer bears witness to this fact.

middle. Its name comes from the four cypresses adorning it, now hundreds of years old, or from the railings placed in it to connect the *Sala de la Barca* (Boat Room) with the Emperor's Rooms.

LINDARAJA COURTYARD

This courtyard is an Italian style garden with a Renaissance fountain in the centre with a white marble basin. It is just below the *Lindaraja Mirador*, which is where it gets its name from, and it is next to the *Courtyard of the Railings*. This landscaped courtyard is the result of the work carried out by Charles V and it involved enclosing the Lindaraja area, which had been open with views of the Albaycin and the valley.

THE QUEEN'S BOUDOIR

The *Peinador de la Reina* is a very lovely mirador next to the *Emperor's Rooms*. The name comes from the fact that the Empress Isabella transformed it into a dressing room. It was also used later by Isabella of Parma, Philip V's wife. It is located in the top part of an Arab tower, which Yusuf I, also called Abul-Hachach, had built. That is why this tower is also known as the **Tower of Abul-Hachach.** According to tradition, this tower was used by the sultan as a place to relax and give parties in. *The Boudoir* (which is not always open to the public) is decorated inside with fresco paintings by the Italian painters Julio Aquiles and Alejandro Mayner, who painted Renaissance scenes of metamorphosis in animals and plants and other allegorical scenes of Charles V's expedition to La Goleta, Tunisia and Sicily.

COURTYARD OF THE RAILINGS OR THE CYPRESSES

The *Patio de la Reja* or de *los Cipreses* is accessed from an overhead passageway built in Christian times to connect the harem with the *Salón de Embajadores* (Hall of Ambassadors) and it provides an excellent view of the Albaycin, Sacromonte and the Darro Valley. It is a secluded and elegant Italian style courtyard with a small fountain in the

Left:
Detail of the secluded Courtyard of the Railings or the Cypresses.

Bottom:
Lindaraja Courtyard.

Left:
*Detail of the stuccoes
in the Rest Room.*

Right:
King's Bath in the Plunge Pool Room.

The Royal Baths

They were built in the reign of Yusuf I (1333-1354). They are not always open to the public for preservation reasons, but they are extremely interesting due to the important role and meaning they played in Arab life. They are also known as the *Baths of Comares Palace*, since they are part of it. In Nasrid times, they were accessed through one of the doors next to the Boat Room, in the *Patio de los Arrayanes* (Courtyard of the Myrtles). The current entrance, through the lower floor, is a Christian alteration.

Bathing is a religious obligation for Arabs, since the Koran makes bodily cleanliness obligatory in order to have spiritual cleanliness. Arab baths are a copy of the Roman thermal ones, although they are smaller and generally adapted to the requirements of a house or palace. We know there were many baths in the complex of the Alhambra and some of them were public, such as those that were next to the Mosque. Others were private. The norm was for every important house or palace to have its own baths, so the Generalife and the Palace of the Lions must have had some. However, even though research has proved they were once there, they do not exist today. The reason why nearly all the baths in the Alhambra disappeared lies in the fact that they were forbidden by Royal Warrant after the Reconquest,

as Christians considered them to be malicious and a symbol of Muslim religious practices. If the only ones to have survived are in *Comares Palace* then this is due to the fact that they were adapted for the personal use of Charles V.

As already mentioned above, Muslims based their baths on the structure of the Roman thermal ones, with slight modifications. Normally they are divided into four rooms, which are also to be found in Roman baths: "apoditerium", which is a dry room, for changing clothes or for resting after the bath; "frigidarium", "tepidarium" and "caldarium", which are the three bath or wet rooms in the strict sense of the term, with water, high temperatures and steam in the atmosphere. The big difference is in the "frigidarium" or cold room, as in the Alhambra more than one room would be a kind of hall

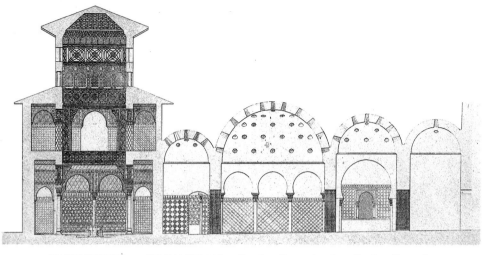

REST ROOM (APODITERIUM)   COLD ROOM (FRIGIDARIUM)   STEAM ROOM (TEPIDARIUM)   PLUNGE POOL ROOM (CALDARIUM)

Top:
Drawing by Owen showing the different rooms forming the structure of the baths.

where there was no cold water pool as the Roman "frigidarium" had. Instead there was a small basin for ablutions. The "tepidarium" was a warm washing and massage room and the "caldarium" was a heated room for the hot plunge bath. Right next to the latter room, separated by a narrow wall, were the furnaces and the boiler, where the water and air were heated.

In medieval times there were only two doors to enter the baths from outside, and they belonged to independent sectors that were not connected. One was used by the bathers, which has already been mentioned, and it was inside the palace in the *Courtyard of the Myrtles* (later changed by the Christians). The other was the door to the furnace and it was down below next to the west gallery of *Lindaraja Courtyard*. It was used by the personnel who kept the boiler hot. The Christians were responsible for some more alterations. The most important was that they made some openings for doors, thus weakening the bath's primitive insulation, which is so necessary to prevent losses of hot air and to protect privacy. Below is a description of each one of the rooms.

REST ROOM

This was the "changing and rest room" ("apoditerium"). Public baths did not have this room, or at least they were not as important and sumptuous as those in the royal baths. This room leads onto the baths. There are lanterns or divans on both sides of the room in side niches. These beds or supports were covered with cushions and covers and were where the royal family rested after bathing. They undressed here at the beginning and returned after the bath was finished to rest, talk with the women in the harem or just be alone. They even had something to eat there, as they could be in the baths for a long time. It is one of the most restored rooms in the Alhambra, and the walls have been polychromed again, although perhaps the colours are not the same as those used originally.

Its most peculiar feature is that it has two floors. Groups of musicians and singers recited verses or played instruments in the top gallery. According to legend, they were blind so that they could not see the ladies naked. Groups of dancers (odalisques) danced in the courtyard. Bathers got undressed here and covered their bodies with light white fabrics, especially their heads and shoulders, and they also put on slippers with wooden soles before entering the bath area, since

Top:
*Rest Room. It has two floors and it is one
of the most restored rooms in the Alhambra.*

the floor was hot. According to Gallego and
Burín, the legends also mention that the sultan
used the top gallery to pick the lady he wanted to
spend that night with, which he did by throwing
an apple down to her. Although this *Rest Room*
has been heavily restored, the rest is virtually
intact. The large copper boiler to heat the water
was even still in place at the end of the 18th century.
Unlike this first room, which is richly decorated,
the next ones are much more moderate. They
also have vaulted ceilings, with eight-pointed star-
shaped holes to let the light through.

COLD ROOM

This was the first of the bathing or steam
rooms. However, it was not a real "frigidarium",
but rather a kind of acclimatisation hall for the
other hotter rooms. It did not have the cold pool
of the Roman thermae. Instead, this was replaced
by a small basin used for partial ablutions. As the
Koran says, before praying, you have to bathe:
"wash your eyes to your forehead, mouth to your
neck, hands to your elbows and feet to your
ankles". In other words, every part of the body
that for Muslims can sin. The small door on one
of the sides must have been the entrance to a
toilet.

STEAM ROOM

This room ("tepidarium") had to remain closed
so that the steam could not escape to the previous
room. The door that is currently set in the east
wall did not exist in medieval times, as this would
have involved losing heat. It is the central room
and the longest and most important in the baths.
The star-shaped skylights in the vaults were
covered by coloured glass, water ran through
the channels in the floor and the marble was
heated by underground channels, producing an
abundance of steam. There were alcoves on both
sides, separated from the central space by three
arches, where it is assumed they sat or lay down
to be massaged.

PLUNGE POOL ROOM

This was the hot room ("caldarium"). There
are two compartments here, one on each side
and they both have a basin, one for the hot bath

and the other for the cold bath. The basin known as the *Sultana's Bath* is in the compartment on the right. The one in the compartment on the left is larger and it is known as the *Sultan's Bath*. Above it there is a niche with an inscription dedicated to the builder of these rooms, Yusuf I. Two taps provided the cold and hot water. This room is next to the furnace, so it must have been the one that reached the highest temperatures. In fact, in the centre, the south wall (the one touching the furnace) is much thinner so that the most heat possible would pass through. The inside temperature probably reached fifty degrees centigrade.

The steam in the atmosphere opened pores and to encourage this process they rubbed their bodies with horsehair, soaping themselves afterwards. Finally they stood up in the bath, pouring water over themselves. After they had finished the entire process, they returned to the first room where they would rest as described above.

FURNACE FACILITIES

These facilities were not connected with the rest of the baths, not only to stop the smoke passing through to the bath areas, but also so that the workers in the furnace, woodcutters and other people, who were not personnel serving at the palace (such as those working in the bath areas), would not be able to access them. Besides, the constant toing and froing involved in tasks like cutting wood, storing it or feeding the boiler would have disturbed the atmosphere of peace and quiet of the rooms in the baths. However, there was an underground link between the furnace and the "caldarium". This link was the "hypocaust", an underground channel that hot air circulated through from the furnace, heating the marble floor of the "caldarium". The boiler was fed with aromatic wood.

The entrance to these facilities from outside the palace was at the end of the street called *calle de los leñadores* (of the woodcutters), which no longer exists. This street disappeared as "urban space" when the rooms of the Palace of Charles V were built. Part of it went through what is today the west gallery of *Lindaraja Courtyard,* which is where the baths are currently visited from.

Right:
Steam Room. It is the central and largest room of them all.

THE PARTAL AND

The Towers

*Long ago, beautiful residences,
homes to the most distinguished
families in the Alhambra,
stood in this area of the monument.
This is also where the most splendid
towers are, which are so richly
decorated that they are like small
palaces inside.*

L ong ago this part of the Alhambra was the area in the city inhabited by the most distinguished families. In former times, fine residences and beautiful palaces stood in the area now covered by these gardens and today, apart from the *Palacio del Partal* (Partal Palace), which is also known as the *Torre de las Damas* (Tower of the Ladies), the small oratory and some houses, only some ruins and traces of them remain. This is the location of the most splendid towers in the whole complex of the Alhambra, facing the Albaycin. They are more like palatial rooms designed for living in and for enjoying the view than for defending the city.

The Partal's gardens do not date back to Muslim times, as they were created more recently. When this area of the complex was excavated and researched remains of buildings were found whose walls and incomplete floors were not much more than a metre high. This is the reason why the decision was made to landscape the area, perhaps to avoid the sad sight of some dry ruins, and to put water back into what remained of the ponds, small channels and fountains discovered. The purpose of these gardens was therefore to embellish and condition some archaeological remains, which in Muslim times housed the palaces and residences of the Nasrid aristocracy. (Jesús Bermúdez Pareja. Cuadernos de la Caja de Ahorros: *El Partal y la Alhambra Alta).*

Left:
*Partal Palace or the
Tower of the Ladies.*

Top right:
*Partal Pond
and Gardens.*

Bottom right:
*Detail of the Portico of
the Tower of the Ladies.*

PARTAL PALACE
(TOWER OF THE LADIES)

This is the oldest palace preserved in the Alhambra, dating from the times of Muhammad III (1302-1309). Its name comes from the Arabic word *Partal*, which means "portico", as this is its most outstanding architectural feature. Since the 16th century it has also been known by the name of *Torre de las Damas* (Tower of the Ladies). The fact that it has a tower, a five-arched portico and a pond points towards the possibility of it having been the palace at one time. We still do not know exactly whether there were side bays or walls enclosing all the space around the pond.

There are three well differentiated spaces: the *arched portico*, with a wooden ceiling that is well worth looking up at; the *hall* at the back, where there are the remains of the tiled surround of the lower part of the walls and the *top mirador* or *"palomar"*, with plasterwork that

is as old as it is beautiful and therefore extremely valuable. The ceiling of this mirador, a cupola made of carved wood, is a copy. The original was sold to the tower's last private owner, a German called Gwinner, and it is currently in the Islamisches Museum in Berlin. The inside of the mirador is not usually open to the public.

THE ORATORY

It is located next to the *Tower of the Ladies*. It is a small independent construction, with two side windows affording beautiful views of the landscapes surrounding it. Some people think this is strange, since the beauty surrounding it outside may distract from prayer. However, we must not forget that for Muslims nature represents the existence of God and Paradise. Inside it is very splendid and formed by five panels representing the five pillars of Islam. In the centre is the Mihrah, a horseshoe arch, with three golden shells above it.

PALACE OF YUSUF III

There are only a few remains of this palace, located in the area known as *Upper Partal*. However, we do know that it was the largest and most important palace in the Alhambra, after the palaces forming the Royal Residence. It was built by Yusuf III (1408-1417). In Christian times, the Catholic Monarchs gave it to the first Governor of the Alhambra, Iñigo de Mendoza, who had the titles of Marquis of Mondéjar and Count of Tendilla, which is why the palace is also known by these two names.

The first thought that comes to mind is to wonder how a building of such beauty and size could almost completely disappear. The reason for this is that during the succession conflict for the crown of Spain between the Bourbons and the Hapsburgs, the descendants of the Count of Tendilla gave their support to the House of Austria. That is why the Bourbons, when they finally came to the throne, took the governorship of the Alhambra and the rights over this Palace away from this family in reprisal. In turn, the Tendillas decided to destroy it, so that no-one else could ever occupy it again.

Among the ruins still standing you can see the remains of the main courtyard among the gardens. The dimensions of its pool, which are similar to the one in the *Patio de los Arrayanes* (Courtyard of the Myrtles), give us an idea of the importance and size that this palace had. The size of the remains of what were its baths also indicate the fact that they must have been part of a large construction.

THE TOWERS

Not all the towers in the complex will be referred to here. There are at least twenty-two (originally there were more than thirty). This section will concentrate on those in this area, facing the Generalife and the Albaycin, specifically the *Torre de los Picos* (Tower of the Points), the *Torre de la Cautiva* (Tower of the Captive Lady) and the *Torre de las Infantas* (Tower of the Princesses). The last two are like small palaces and are the most beautiful inside in the Alhambra. For preservation reasons, they are not always open to the public.

– **The Torre de los Picos.** Seen from the outside, it is the most peculiar, since its battlements

Top right:
Tower of the Captive Lady and parapet walk.

Bottom right:
Tower of the Points and
exterior bastion built by the Christians.

Left and bottom:
Details of the outside of the Tower
of the Captive Lady.

Next page:
Inside the Tower of the Captive Lady,
which is like a small palace as
it is so richly decorated.

the best in the Alhambra due to the variety of colours and geometrical drawings and some of the few with inscriptions on their top frieze, such as those in the Lindaraja Mirador. It owes its name to the fact that, according to legend, the Christian lady, Isabel de Solís, later called Zoraya (bright morning star) lived here in isolation. She was the favourite of king Muley Hacem and this love made his legitimate wife, Aixa, jealous and led to the clash between the king and the distinguished Abencerraje family, as they considered that the queen suffered great insult, disregard and humiliation because of this Christian lady.

are shaped like points, which is why it is called the *Tower of the Points*. In Muslim times, it must have been one of the most important towers as it housed the gate for accessing the Generalife from the Alhambra, called the *Puerta del Arrabal* (Gate of the Poor Quarter). It was the only way people could get to and from the Generalife. In Christian times, an exterior bastion was added to it, so the tower and gate are now on the inside. The new outside gate of the bastion was called the *Puerta de Hierro* (Iron Gate). This Christian gate and bastion can be seen from the pathway called the *Cuesta de los Chinos* (Hill of Pebbles).

– The Torre de la Cautiva. The *Tower of the Captive Lady* dates from the times of Yusuf I (1333-1354). This is gathered from the inscriptions in plaster on the surround in the main room, which praise the figure of the king. It is like a small palace inside. Most noteworthy are the rich decoration of its stuccoes and above all the tiled surrounds of the windows, which are some of

– **The Torre de las Infantas.** The *Tower of the Princesses* was built when Muhammad VII (1392-1408) was king of Granada. It is also a small palace with a winding entrance and benches for eunuchs or guards, an inside courtyard with adjacent alcoves and a water fountain in the centre of the room, which is not original. There is a beautiful view of the Generalife from the windows. It is one of the last constructions in the Muslim Alhambra, built in a period of decline, which is reflected in the more simple decoration. The top floor is hardly decorated at all and above it there is a terrace. The original ceiling was muqarna and it disappeared after an earthquake in the 19th century, when it was replaced by the current wooden one. However, the curious vault at the entrance is original. Its name comes from the legend about three Arab princesses living here: Zaida, Zoraida and Zorahaida.

Top:
Detail of the ceiling in the Tower of the Princesses.

Right:
Inside the Tower of the Princesses.
You can see the attractive layout of its rooms.

THE PALACE OF
Charles V

When Charles V came to Granada, he decided to build a Palace in the Renaissance style in the Alhambra, which would be known as the "New Royal Residence".

A s already mentioned earlier in this book, when Charles V came to Granada on his honeymoon, he was enchanted by this city and decided to build a palace in the Alhambra complex, but naturally in line with European mentality. The architect Pedro Machuca, who had studied in Italy as a disciple of Michelangelo, was commissioned with the work and he brought the influence of Renaissance masters with him. It is curious that Machuca, a relatively poor painter, was recommended by the Marquis of Mondéjar for such a large project with so much responsibility. He must have been known for his skills as an architect and his knowledge acquired in Italy. For that reason, he was made to be in Granada to coincide with the Emperor's visit, who met him and commissioned the work to him after seeing the plans. He was immediately given somewhere to work, a place opposite the palace, which is called Machuca Courtyard and Tower.

The work started in 1527. In 1550, when Machuca died, the palace was still unfinished, so his son Luis continued the work. In the reign of Philip II, he was followed by Juan de Orea, who was advised by Juan de Herrera (the creator of the Monastery of El Escorial). Later there were even more, but they were not very important as almost all the work had already been done.

The palace was financed with money collected from the Moriscos, who paid taxes not only to go on living there, but also to be able to continue with their rites and traditions. The amount collected was 80,000 ducats per year, of which 10,000 were for defraying the costs of building the palace. Another part, 6,000 ducats, was taken from the income from the Royal Alcazares of Seville. The amounts obtained from the sentences of convicts in the courts of Granada, Loja and

Previous page: South facade of the Palace of Charles V.

Top left: Detail of the pediment of the door in the south facade.

Top right: Detail of one of the children appearing on the west facade.

Main facade of the Palace of Charles V.

Alhama were also used to finance the project. After the Emperor died, his son Philip II continued the work, but when the Morisco Rebellion broke out, leading to the War of the Alpujarras or of Granada, there were not enough resources and 4,000 ducats of the money collected from Granada sugar was used.

It is very important to establish once and for all that the Palace of Charles V did not destroy any important parts of the Arab Royal Residence or of any of the other constructions in the Alhambra. Only a small part of Comares Palace was destroyed to build the chapel and crypt of the Renaissance palace, which was probably a room similar to the *Sala de la Barca* (Boat Room).

THE OUTSIDE OF THE PALACE

The most important of the palace's four sides are the south and the west ones because of their decoration. The entrance is in the latter, which is where the main facade is, a reflection of the purest Renaissance tradition. It has a door in the centre and two smaller doors on either side of it, between two ionic columns. There are two winged female figures above the central door, reclined on the pediment, which remind us of the Medici tombs, made by Michelangelo. The pediments of the small doors have infants with bunches of fruit and above them are medallions in relief with images of the Battle of Pavia. The bottom part of the palace is designed in a "Tuscan" style, while the top part has details belonging to a "late Renaissance" tradition with touches of Churrigueresque in the excess of fruit clustered together and pomegranates on the pediments and cornices, which are of Ionic style. There are some showy metal rings placed around the palace's entire facade. The majority of the rings are held by lions (royal symbols), except at the corners, where they are held by two eagles on every one, representing the two-headed eagle, the symbol of the Hapsburgs.

The pedestals of the columns of the main facade have bas-reliefs in marble with allegories of triumph, chubby infants holding up the world with the imperial crown, Hercules' columns and the motto "Plus ultra" ("beyond"), adopted by the Spanish monarchs after the discovery of America. These bas-reliefs also depict scenes of the Emperor's war with his rival Francis I of France, namely the Battle of Pavia. The drawings of

Top:
Detail of one of the medallions on the main facade.

Centre:
Pediment of the Palace's main facade.

Bottom:
Detail of the bas-reliefs of the pedestal of the facade's columns.

Previous page:
The Palace's circular courtyard
and double gallery.

Right:
Top gallery of the Palace.

these bas-reliefs were done by Machuca and the marble was carved by Juan de Orea and Leval.

The top part of the facade was done after Machuca's death. The central columns are of Doric style here. There are three medallions hidden in a circle of serpentine (green marble) from the Sierra Nevada. The one in the middle has the coat of arms of Spain and the ones on the sides show scenes of Hercules' twelve labours. One shows Hercules killing the Nemean lion and the other Hercules holding the Cretan bull.

THE CENTRAL COURTYARD

There is an enormous Roman-style circular courtyard inside with two galleries, one placed on top of the other. The bottom gallery has thirty-two Doric style columns and the top one has Ionic style columns. The columns are made of stone called "pudinga" or "almendrilla" from Turro (Loja), a town in Granada. The courtyard probably had a parapet to extract water from a well underneath it in the centre, which was discovered when the courtyard was covered with the paving material it currently has.

Neither does it have the cupola and the vault closing the courtyard, with a central lantern to let light pass through. This vault would have possibly been coffered, just like the one covering the Pantheon in Rome, which was undoubtedly the model Machuca followed to cover the interior. However, the courtyard was never covered, even the roof of the top gallery was not finished at the time and it was completed only a few years ago.

The frieze surrounding the courtyard depicts small ox heads. This decorative motif comes from ancient Greece and Rome where friezes, metopes and sarcophaguses were decorated with scenes of ox sacrifices. These heads are known as "bucrania". Also worth mentioning are the courtyard's wonderful acoustics, which is why the symphony concerts of the "International Music and Dance Festival of Granada" have been held here since modern times. This palace is also the home of two important museums: the **Alhambra Museum** and the **Fine Arts Museum**.

The Generalife

This was a recreational palace and estate, independent of the Alhambra, used by the Nasrid Kings as a place of retreat and rest.

Left:
Detail of some of the roses flourishing here.

Right:
Courtyard of the Water Channel,
seen from the top floor of the South Pavilion.

Bottom:
Generalife Palace and its surroundings.

The Generalife was a recreational estate or garden. It is thought that it was built at the time of Ismail I (1314-1325). It is located on the *Cerro del Sol* (Sun Hill) and it covered a much larger area in those days as it went right up to the neighbouring mountains, almost up to a place known today as the *"Llano de la Perdiz"* (Partridge Plain) and it was guarded by the highest fort in Muslim Granada, the *"Castillo de Santa Elena"* (Saint Helen's Castle) or *"Silla del Moro"* (Seat of the Moor). It was designed to fulfil several purposes: recreation, agriculture and horticulture, livestock raising and game preserve. It was totally enclosed and independent of the Alhambra, with its own guard force. As the idea was to provide somewhere for the kings of Granada to retreat and relax, they made sure that it was as delightful as possible. In the 19th century it was expanded with gardens no less beautiful than the original ones. The Generalife is one of the areas whose original state during the reign of the Nasrid kings has been transformed the most. Its name comes from the Arabic words "Yannat-al-arif", which mean "architect's garden" and

The Generalife

1.- Avenue of the Cypresses
2.- Amphitheatre
3.- New gardens
   (Formerly they were the Huerta Grande
   and Huerta de Fuentepeña)

4.- Huerta Colorá
5.- Courtyard of Dismounting or the Mounting Block
6.- Polo Courtyard
7.- House of Friends
8.- Courtyard of the Water Channel

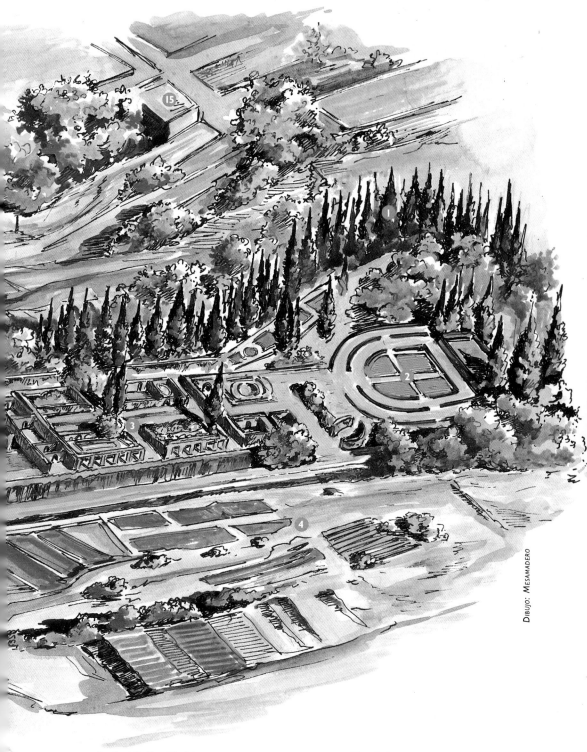

DIBUJO: MESAMADERO

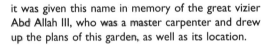

the ticket offices. After going through this gate, you come to a path lined with high cypress trees. This path branches into two. The one on the right is a continuation of the avenue of the cypresses. The one in the centre, which is the one this book follows, leads to the *New Gardens*.

THE NEW GARDENS

These gardens date from 1931. They were replanted in the Second Republic and are Italian in style. Cut cypress trees form walls and labyrinths, with pergolas and rose bushes. There is also an amphitheatre built in 1952, which is used for concerts and performances in the International Music and Dance Festival of Granada. In the centre of these gardens there is a pool with water lilies floating on the surface, where fountains and cypresses alternate. Ahead and to the left of you along the path are wonderful views of the Alhambra and the city.

THE GENERALIFE *HUERTAS*

All of the Generalife was surrounded by *huertas* (orchards and cultivated fields), which supplied the Alhambra. Some of them have

it was given this name in memory of the great vizier Abd Allah III, who was a master carpenter and drew up the plans of this garden, as well as its location.

It was private property, independent of the Alhambra, as the Catholic Monarchs gave it to commander Gil Vázquez Rengifo, who was appointed governor of the Generalife. The last private owner was the Marquis of Campotéjar and in 1925 it became the property of the State, becoming part of the Alhambra and Generalife Trust.

The Generalife can be accessed from several parts of the monument: the main entrance, which is next to the ticket offices; from the control point next to the San Francisco Parador, along the path in the Secano area; or going along the path between the Partal and the Towers, at the end of this area. The route described here starts from the main entrance next to

now disappeared and the most recent gardens in the complex were planted instead. Others still exist and are still cultivated: **Huerta de la Mercería** (Haberdashery), in the top part, of which today only gardens are preserved, and the "Albercón de las Damas" (Reservoir of the Ladies), which supplies the gardens and flows towards the Alhambra after collecting water from the "Acequia del Tercio" (Irrigation Channel). **Huerta Colorá** (Red), which is located down below on the left, opposite the *Torre de los Picos* (Tower of the Points) and still used. **Huerta Grande** (Large), which continued on from *Huerta Colorá*, covered the area known today as the *New Gardens*. **Huerta de Fuentepeña** (Rock Spring), which also covered some of the site of the *New Gardens and the Amphitheatre*. It had a gate for the King's flocks to pass through called the *"Postigo de los Carneros"* (Side Gate of the Rams). This *huerta* is called *fuentepeña* because it had a spring rising out of a rock, with a basin used as a water trough by the livestock. The two lower *huertas* (*Grande* and *Fuentepeña*) are separated from the top one (*Mercería*) by the avenues of the *Cypresses* and of the *Oleanders*. For the precise location of these *huertas*, please see the layout in the drawing of the Generalife illustrating these pages.

Left:
Central pool in the New Gardens.

Centre:
View of the New Gardens.

Right:
Huerta Colorá, the only one of the Generalife's huertas that has survived to present day.

Bottom:
Detail of one of the fountains embellishing the New Gardens.

GENERALIFE PALACE

This palace is the focal point of the entire complex. Over the years it has become very disfigured and transformed, but in Muslim times it was a genuine royal residence, with all the conveniences and elements required for the accommodation of the Nasrid monarchs. There is a real Muslim garden, as mentioned by Ibn Luyun in his "Treatise on Agriculture", in which he says: "You should choose a hillock that is easy to guard and protect. The building must

face midday, at the entrance to the estate, and the well and the pool must be installed as high as possible, or rather than a well, open up a channel running through the shade. The residence must have two doors so that it is more protected and he who inhabits it can rest more" (this is very different from the Christian phrase: "a house with two doors is difficult to guard").

Ibn Luyun continues to say: "Plant clumps of bushes next to the pool, which will always be green and a delight to your eyes (...) Surround the estate with vines and plant rose bushes along the avenues crossing it. The rest of the estate, at a certain distance from the vines, is for tillage fields (...) Plant fig and other similar trees along the borders. All the fruit trees must be planted in the north part, so that they protect the rest of the estate from the wind. In the centre of the estate there must be a pavilion surrounded by seats, providing views on all sides, but in such a

way that whoever enters the pavilion cannot hear what is being said by those inside it, making sure that whoever goes towards it does not go unnoticed (...) The estate will be enclosed with a wall to protect it".

"The stable for animals and for farming implements must be located near the entrance (...) the stables for sheep and cattle must be in the lowest part of the building, very close so that they can be watched over easily (...) Workers must be young and make sure they heed the advice of their elders".

The reason why Ibn Luyun has been quoted is because nobody can give us a better and truer idea of the Hispano-Muslim garden than he does in his "Treatise on Agriculture", written in Almeria in 749 in the Muslim age. It was translated into Spanish by Joaquina Eguaras Ibáñez (Alhambra Trust) in 1957.

It is interesting to note that in the Nasrid age, you had to go through the ramparts of the Alhambra to go to the Generalife, possibly through the *Puerta del Arrabal* (Gate of the Poor Quarter), located at the foot of the *Torre de los Picos* (Tower of the Points). The route followed went down the gully along the "Cuesta de los Chinos" (Hill of Pebbles) and then went up again along a walled path, which went through the *Huertas Colorá* and *Grande*. The Nasrid nobility usually accessed the Generalife through two adjoining courtyards, the anterooms of the palace. The first one is the **Patio del Descabalgamiento** or **del Apeadero** (Courtyard of Dismounting or the Mounting Block) since it is assumed that the emirs came from the Alhambra on horseback and dismounted here. That is why there are blocks for dismounting and a water trough.

Previous page:
Courtyard of the Water Channel
and North Pavilion. (Photograph taken before the courtyard's garden was overhauled in 2003).

Top:
Entrance to Generalife Palace.

Right:
Courtyard prior to the Palace.

The next courtyard, adorned with orange trees, is beautiful and it has a small fountain in the centre. There is a rectangular door here with a lintel, tiled green and black on a white background, similar to those on the *Facade of Comares Room*, which takes you inside the palace. Among the green ceramics of the doorframe is the symbol of the key, which appears on other doors in the Alhambra. Once inside the Palace, you come across the following: the *Patio de la Acequia* (Courtyard of the Water Channel), the *Pabellón Sur* (South Pavilion), the *Pabellón Norte* (North Pavilion) and the *Patio de la Sultana* (Courtyard of the Sultana).

– **The Courtyard of the Water Channel.** It is in the middle of the palace and there is a water channel running longitudinally through it, which the entire courtyard is arranged around. In the *west part* there is a gallery with eighteen arches with a mirador in the middle. The symbols of the Catholic Monarchs, the yoke and arrows, and the words *"tanto monta"* (which

mean "it makes no difference, either Isabella or Ferdinand") are painted on the jambs of the arches. From this gallery you can see the *Huerta Colorá*, the *Torre de la Cautiva* (Tower of the Captive Lady), the *Torre de las Infantas* (Tower of the Princesses) and the entire complex of monuments of the Alhambra with the city in the background. The construction of the **east wing** is new, as a fire destroyed nearly all this wing in 1958. It is thought that the baths, which were no doubt somewhere in this palace, must have been in this wing. These baths do not exist today because, as mentioned in the section on the baths, they were destroyed along with many others in the Alhambra.

– **The South Pavilion.** This may have been the area in the palace used as the harem. It has been greatly modified. The original plaster arches of its portico were replaced by brick ones. The views seen from its top mirador are superb. Adjoining this pavilion, on the outside and south side (down below) are the remains of a construction that was part of the palace complex: the **Casa de los Amigos** (the House of Friends). We have learnt its name and use from the advice Ibn Luyun gives in his "Treatise on Agriculture": "A room must be built in the lowest part of the gardens for guests and friends, with an independent door and a small pool hidden by trees from the gaze of those above".

– **The North Pavilion.** This was used as the King's rooms, and it is without a doubt the most interesting part of the entire palace. It has a more traditional layout, with a portico with five arches, the one in the middle being much wider than the side ones. It is the entrance to a triple-arched doorway leading to the *Sala Regia* (Regal Room). There is an inscription on the panels of the three arches giving information on the date of construction (1319, when Ismail I was the emir). This pavilion connects with the **Courtyard of the Sultana.**

– **The Courtyard of the Sultana.** The *Patio de la Sultana* has this name because, according to legend, the sultan saw his favourite kiss an Abencerraje nobleman under the old cypress tree, which is now petrified. In the centre there is a Christian fountain built on top of a small pool. The plants are oleanders, ivies and cypresses. There is also a grotto, where water falls. It is important to note that the water jets in both this courtyard and the Courtyard of the Water Channel do not date from the Muslim age.

Left:
Courtyard of the Water Channel and South Pavilion.
(Photograph taken before the courtyard's garden was overhauled in 2003).

Top left:
Fountain in the Upper Gardens.

Top right:
Courtyard of the Sultana.

Bottom:
Water Staircase.

Next page:
Central pool of the Courtyard of the Water Channel. (Photograph taken before 2003 overhaul).

THE UPPER GARDENS

These gardens are accessed by going through a gate, which has lions and the coat of arms of the Mendoza, in the *Courtyard of the Sultana*. After climbing some stairs, you come to a level higher than that of *Generalife Palace*. In the past this was an olive grove and today you can find magnolias, fir trees, cypresses, an enormous cedar tree and aromatic plants, such as myrtles, jasmines and rose bushes. The most outstanding feature of these gardens is perhaps the very splendid **Water Staircase**, with its vault of laurel trees. The water runs down the banisters as if it were a torrent, since they are hollow and were formerly decorated with tiles. The flowing water acts as a balustrade. The staircase is divided into three sections decorated with circular pools with small fountains. The staircase leads to a modern building of no interest called **Mirador Romántico** (Romantic Mirador), built in 1836. These gardens lead to the exit along the **Paseo de las Adelfas** (Avenue of Oleanders), which has a floral vault. It connects with the **Paseo de los Cipreses** (Avenue of the Cypresses), planted during the time of Isabella II. This is the path that was on our right when we started the route followed in this chapter.

The Albaycin

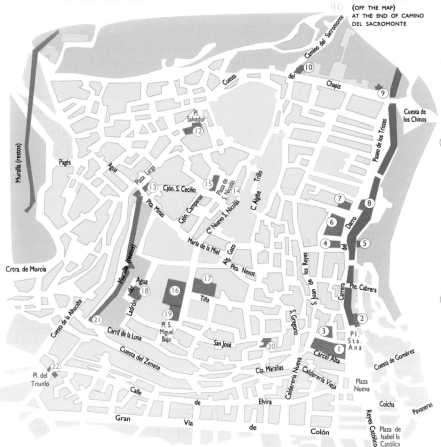

(11) (OFF THE MAP)
AT THE END OF CAMINO
DEL SACROMONTE

MAP OF THE ALBAYCIN

USEFUL INFORMATION:

– As many of the documents in the
Albaycin are not usually open to the public (those with a
sign after them), they can only be viewed by organising the visit with
the institution running them beforehand or on a guided visit for groups.

– The rest of the monuments are regularly open to the public or they can at
least be visited during times of worship.

View of the Albaycin with the Sierra Nevada in the background.

Introduction

Universally known, it is full of places that remind us of this city's Muslim past.

The Albaycin[1] originated as an urban area around the beginning of the 10th century, when the inhabitants of the City of Elvira asked for protection and shelter from Zawi ben Zirí, who was the first of the four kings of the Granadine Zirid dynasty, as a result of the disintegration of the Caliphate and the breaking down of the territory of Al Andalus into minute kingdoms, which very often fought each other.

Medina Elvira (the most important population centre in the area) was located in an open place that was difficult to defend in the event of an attack, so the first thing King Zawi decided to do when he became these people's lord and protector was to find a safer geographical location. This spot was the hill of the Albaycin, where the remains of a former fortress, which had been built by the previous Visigoth settlers, already stood. Its natural beauty also made this a privileged site: streams brimming with running water, rich vegetation and the Sierra Nevada as a backdrop. The inhabitants of Elvira therefore abandoned their insecure city on the slopes of the Sierra Elvira and came to live here. This was the birth of the Albaycin as an important urban area, the origin of what is today the city of Granada.

King Zawi fortified the former *alcazaba* (fortress) and he built some high ramparts.

Sheltered by them, the recently arrived population built a lovely city, which gradually attracted more and more inhabitants from other lands in search of the prosperity and safety this new place offered them. They built cisterns, mosques, large houses and palaces. The most important of them all was the Palace of King Badis, the third Zirid king, which unfortunately no longer exists.

After the Zirids, the Almoravids and the Almohads came to power. This was an age of highs and lows. In 1238, al-Ahmar became the King of Granada, establishing the Nasrid monarchy. At first, he and his court were based in the Albaycin, living in the Palace of King Badis. However, he soon decided to move away from here to the hill opposite, Sabika hill, because he thought it was safer for his family and his court to be far away from the intrigues and treachery the previous kings of Granada were subjected to in the Albaycin's streets. From then on, the king and nobility lived in the "palatine city of the Alhambra" and the people lived in the Albaycin, on the top of

[1] Albaycin may come from the Arabic "Al baezan", which means a district of inhabitants from the city of Baeza (Jaen), as they took refuge here when Baeza fell into the hands of the Christians, in the 13th century. Another less generalised meaning comes from the word "Al bayyazín", which means a quarter of the falconers, since at one time there were a lot of residents who worked in falconry.

One of the many places in the Albaycin where you can see the Alhambra from.

Carrera del Darro in Lower Albaycin.

A typical narrow street in the Albaycin with cobbled paving.

the hill and on its slopes, right up to Granada's limits, which ended a little beyond the square called Plaza Bibarrambla.

In this Nasrid period, the Albaycin continued to grow and prosper and more people came to live here. It became so built up that around 1494 the German traveller Munzer calculated that the population was around 30,000. Its alleys were extremely narrow, under eaves that touched each other and through which hardly any sunlight could pass. It was full of small houses, dirty on the outside, but clean inside, with water cisterns and two pipes, one for drinking water and the other for latrines. Houses that were simple and austere on the outside, but which had beautiful courtyards with flowers, fruit trees and pools inside. These were the origin of the future Granadine "carmens"[2]. They were inhabited by cultured people, most of them craftsmen or small tradesmen: masons, weavers, tailors, esparto craftsmen, shoemakers... A large number of the residents were involved in agriculture as their second activity besides their trade, since it was usual for families to have a garden or a plot of land to cultivate.

When the Catholic Monarchs conquered Granada, the mosques in the Albaycin were converted into churches and some Christians moved into the area. However, the Moors continued to characterise the quarter with the same way of life and idiosyncrasy as before. The number of them living here even increased, as they came to flee the pressure they were under in other parts of the kingdom. However, the persecution, and final expulsion of the Moors in the reign of Phillip III, between 1609-1616, reduced the population to almost a tenth. They had to leave their homes and the Albaycin was left deserted and desolate. Many houses were pulled down, sometimes to widen streets, and others to make bigger plots, bought at a very low price by numerous religious orders and Christian nobles, who built new convents and splendid houses. The depopulation of the quarter was such a problem that the Crown even got involved so that new inhabitants came from other places to repopulate it. But the new settlers did not have the same training as the Moors, neither were they craftsmen. They were humble people, who, instead of helping to rebuild the district, made it even poorer.

The French occupation in the 19th century and above all Mendizábal's Disentailment, involving the confiscation of the property and works of art religious orders had in their convents, were a further setback for the Albaycin. But the most devastating event for the many artistic treasures still housed in this quarter was the burning of the most of its churches and some of its convents in the Second Republic and start of the Spanish Civil War (1931-1936): the churches of San Luis (St. Louis), Salvador (Our Saviour), San Nicolás (St. Nicholas), San Cristóbal (St. Christopher) and some others were burnt and either partly or almost completely destroyed.

In spite of the harsh way the Albaycin has been treated by history, it is still a magical place. Its aromas, sounds, light and the view of its neighbouring Alhambra with the Sierra Nevada in the background make it one of the most different and unique places in the world. (Reference: *Albayzín-solar de reyes,* by Gabriel Pozo Felguera).

[2] Carmen comes from the Arabic word "karm", which means vine. In other words, it was originally an orchard with vineyards. The Granadine carmen is therefore a house with an orchard on a very small scale, used as a private home, full of plants and aromatic flowers, although vines were the dominant feature at first.

Royal Chancery.

Church of Santa Ana

Lower Albaycin

Bathed by the River Darro, it is one of those spots that make Granada a magical city.

The Albaycin is divided into the upper and lower quarter. This division depends on how near each is to the rest of the city and therefore how accessible it is. This lower neighbourhood, as it is only five minutes on foot from the cathedral area (the city centre), is a lovely short walk that is a must for any visitor to Granada. The main streets belonging to this lower Albaycin area are: on the west side, Calle Elvira until it ends in the square called Plaza Nueva, including Calle Calderería, with its teahouses and Moorish craftwork shops. The distinct Muslim character of this street is a recent development. On the south side, the squares Plaza Nueva and Santa Ana and the streets Carrera del Darro and Paseo de los Tristes. Parallel to the latter is Calle San Juan de los Reyes, as the limit to this lower part. The map included in this chapter shows all the streets and squares forming the itinerary of this lower area of the quarter.

Lets start off our stroll in the central and typical Granadine squares **Plaza Nueva** and **Santa Ana,** which are virtually joined together. The first contains the splendid building of the **Real Chancillería** (Royal Chancery), which Phillip II had built as the new headquarters of the High Court of Justice. The Courts of Justice of Granada, as well as those of Andalusia, Extremadura, Murcia, the Mancha and the Canary Islands, were dependent on this Chancery, which the Catholic Monarchs had ordered to be established in Granada. The exterior facade, in Renaissance style and dating from the second half of the 16th century, is by Juan de la Vega and Martín Navarrete. It is divided into two large sections. The bottom one is dominated by three beautiful doors. Above the largest door, the one in the centre, is a cartouche referring to how Phillip II embellished this palace so that it would not be an unworthy seat of his justice. The most striking part of the second section is the

On the whole page:
- *Carrera del Darro covered with snow.*
- *A view of Carrera del Darro.*
- *Remains of the former Cadí Bridge.*

large central window, crowned by Spain's coat of arms, with the statues of the cardinal virtues, Justice and Fortitude, on either side. Inside, it is arranged around a very beautiful courtyard, which may have been designed by Diego de Siloé. Surrounding the courtyard is a double colonnade. Last in this short description of the building is the staircase, financed by the amount of a fine that the magistrates gave the Marquis of Salar for not taking his hat off before them as a sign of respect. It reminds us of the Palace of Charles V, and it is an architectural wonder.

On one side of the neighbouring square, **Plaza de Santa Ana**, is the **Pilar del Toro** (Fountain of the Bull), which is worth noting as the last work of art made by the genius Diego de Siloé. The square is dominated by the **Church of Santa Ana** (St. Anne and former "Jima de Almanzor"[1]), whose tower was a minaret. A belfry was added to it later. Its exquisite doorway, designed by Sebastián Alcántara, in a Renaissance style, is crowned by images of St. Anne and Mary Jacobi and Mary Salome on either side, with a medallion of the Madonna and Child as a finishing piece. The coats of arms on the spandrels of the arch belong

to Archbishop Niño de Guevara. There is only one nave inside with a wooden *laceria*[2] ceiling. The church contains an interesting art collection, including: a Via Dolorosa, a Christ in the Tomb and a St. Bartholomew, by José de Mora; a retable consecrated to Our Lady of the Roses, with a Flemish origin, and Our Lady of Hope, by Risueño.

At the entrance to **Carrera del Darro** there is a house called **Casa de las Pisas** in the street with the same name, Calle de las Pisas. This is where St. John of God died and nowadays it is an interesting museum, with items on display that have been brought here by brothers of this Order from all over the world: ivory and marquetry objects, paintings, small sculptures, etc. **Carrera del Darro** is one of the most picturesque streets in Granada, recreated many a time in drawings and paintings by romantic travellers and painters over the ages. Strolling alongside the River Darro with the Alhambra above as your companion is one of the most beautiful walks you can find in this city. The

[1] Each quarter had a small mosque called a "Jima". The jimas were smaller and less important than the main mosques, such as those that were located on the site of the Church of Sagrario (Tabernacle), Salvador (Our Saviour) or Santa María (St. Mary) in the Alhambra. In 1501, Cardinal Cisneros ordered all the jimas and main mosques in Granada to be turned into parochial churches.
[2] Muslim artwork of regular patterns of straight lines crossing each other.

street as it is today dates from after the Reconquest. In Arab times there were ramparts parallel to the river. The Christians built convents and stately homes here, mainly in the 16th and 17th centuries. After passing the second of the bridges crossing the river, you come across the public baths called **Bañuelo** or **Baño del Nogal**. There were many more of them in the area, but as happened in the Alhambra, they were destroyed by the Christians. Luckily, these baths have survived to this day, albeit deteriorated and very restored. They date from the Zirid age, the 11th century. They are accessed via a Christian tenement house, which was built on top of them. Their structure is very similar to those in the Alhambra, but with the logical differences between public baths and those for the private use of the royal family. As a result, they have a small room or vestibule used as a changing room instead of the rest room that the baths in the Alhambra have. The largest room is the *tepidarium* or warm washing room. Hot water ran through the middle part and the beds for the massages were on the sides. The capitals of the columns are very interesting. There are some dating from the caliphal age, in the 10th century, which are mixed with others from the 11th century and some in a Byzantine style. Next is the *caldarium* or hot room and the furnace facilities are at the end.

Opposite these baths are the remains of the bridge called **Puente de Cadí**, which must have been very important and much used in the Nasrid age, since it linked the Albaycin with the Alhambra. Further up the street is the **Convent of Santa Catalina de Zafra** (St. Catherine), which owes its name to Hernando de Zafra, the Catholic Monarchs' secretary, who financed the convent and gave some houses he owned so that it could be founded on them in 1520. This is one of the many convents in the Albaycin, but unfortunately, in the majority of the cases, it is impossible to visit them. Just some of the churches, during times of worship. Luckily, this is not the case of the next building, the **Casa de Castril,** which belonged to Hernando de Zafra's family. Its exceptional doorway, in a Plateresque style (1539), is the best indication of the nobility and importance of the family that owned this palace. The most curious of the elements it contains is a small "Comares Tower", the coat of arms the Catholic Monarchs granted the Zafra family as a payment for their services. Another detail

On the whole page:
- *Outside view of the Casa de Castril, the home of the Archaeological Museum.*
- *Courtyard inside the museum.*
- *Bañuelo or Nogal Baths, warm washing room.*

worth mentioning in the facade is the blocked off window on one of the corners, where the following is engraved into the stone: "hoping for it in heaven", and there is a well-known legend in Granada about it [3]. Inside the building is one of the most important museums in the city, the **Provincial Archaeological Museum**, whose varied and valuable collection is well worth a visit. Directly opposite is the **Church of San Pedro y San Pablo** (St. Peter and St. Paul). It was designed by Juan de Maeda and construction was completed in 1567. It would appear that the "Mosque of the Baths" stood here previously. It was replaced by another church, which was pulled down in 1559 to build this one. A little further on is the **Convent of San Bernardo** (St. Bernhard), dating from the beginning of the 19th century.

This brief itinerary of the lower part of the Albaycin ends in **Paseo de los Tristes**, one of the most charming places in the world, with the view of the Alhambra as a constant backdrop. It was formerly called the "Paseo de la Puerta de Guadix", but its current name, which translates as the Avenue of the Sorrowful, comes from the fact that all funeral processions on the way to the cemetery passed along this street and it was here that the cortège said farewell to the deceased, who went on to the cemetery along the Cuesta de los Chinos accompanied only by those closest to him. This was a very busy site in the past, where bullfights were held. The climb up to Sacromonte and upper Albaycin starts here, along **Cuesta del Chapiz**. This hill is the location of **Córdova Palace**, which, although it is difficult to believe, is a reconstruction made using the preserved architectural elements of the former palace, which was somewhere else, behind Plaza Isabel la Católica. The houses known as **Casas del Chapiz** are a little further up, on the corner with Camino del Sacromonte. They are Moorish buildings dating from the beginning of the 16th century and are currently the headquarters of the School of Arabic Studies.

Top:
Church of San Pedro.

Bottom left:
Córdova Palace.

Bottom right:
Pool in the Chapiz Houses.

[3] According to the legend, the lord of the house entered his daughter's bedroom one day and found her half undressed and his most loyal page hidden in the room. As an excuse, the page said that he was there because he had gone to help her, surprising one of her lovers in the process, who had jumped out of the window when he saw him. The Lord of Zafra did not believe him: "If that is the truth, then you are his accomplice!" he reproached him. As things were looking bleak, the page begged for mercy and justice. The lord replied: "HOPE FOR IT IN HEAVEN! Tomorrow you will be hanged from that balcony." The servant was hanged and the balcony was blocked off for ever.

Sacromonte with the Alhambra and the city in the background.

Sacromonte

Gypsies came to live here in the 18th century, excavating their homes in caves. Since then it has become a singular and legendary place.

Halfway up Cuesta del Chapiz is the road called **Camino del Sacromonte**, well-known as the former gypsy quarter. The "Egyptian tribes", as the gypsies were known in the age of the Catholic Monarchs, settled in Granada after the conquest, first in other districts on the outskirts of the city and later, in the 18th century, on the slopes of this hill called the Monte de Valparaíso. Their way of life, their language ("caló"), their fiestas and dances and the fact that they excavated their homes in caves, inspired many a romantic traveller to write about them, and since then many visitors have come to this place, thus further increasing its magic and legend. Today, all that is left of that age are some cave homes, where *zambras* (a flamenco song and dance form) are organised, clearly aimed at tourists. The Ave Maria schools, founded in 1889 by Andrés Manjón so that gypsy and poor children could study, are at the beginning of the road.

At the end of this road, right at the top of Monte de Valparaíso, is the **Sacromonte Abbey and the School**. This Institution was founded here in the 17th century by Pedro de Castro Cabeza de Vaca y Quiñónez, the archbishop of Granada at the time, to commemorate the fact that some sheets of lead, "leaden books", were found in some caves ("the Sacred Caves") here in 1594. These stated that Saints Cecilius (the first archbishop and patron of Granada), Hiscio and Tesifón had been martyred here in 65 AD. Since then, this place has been known as "Sacromonte", which means the "sacred mountain". Part of the school was burned down in a fire, but the Abbey can be visited. It has an important library with over 25,000 volumes.

The large **courtyard**, with a fountain in the middle and twenty-five arches with the founder's coat of arms and the star of Solomon, the symbol of the Institution, is the first thing you visit. Next is the **museum,** with some extremely valuable items, such as "Our Lady of the Roses", a Flemish panel by Gerard David, and three excellent Immaculate Conceptions by Raxis, Sánchez Cotán

Top left:
Outside view of Sacromonte Abbey.

Top right:
Courtyard inside the Abbey.

Bottom:
The church's high altar retable.

and Niño de Guevara. There is also an interesting collection of incunabula, codices and twenty Arabic manuscripts of immeasurable value, as well as vestments, pulpit cloths, altar frontals and chasubles.

The **church**, dating from the start of the 17th century, with extensions made in the two following centuries, has good Baroque retables and ashlar masonry. The high altar retable dates from 1743 and it is attributed to Duque Cornejo. Its most striking elements are the statues of "St. Cecilius" and "St. Tesifón", with their ashes kept underneath them, and a large relief of the "Assumption" in the top section. A small room next to the right side of this retable contains the tomb of the archbishop of Castro, who was buried here with his parents. There is a "Virgin Mary" by Risueño on the altar on the left of the crossing. As far as the rest of the church is concerned, also worth noting among the paintings are: "Apostle St. James" and the "Martyrdom of St. Andrew", and among the sculptures: "Our Lady of the Caves", a small figure dating from the 18th century, "St. Francis Receiving the Stigmata", "St. Anthony with Child" and, in particular, the "Christ of Consolation" or "of the Gypsies", an excellent Christ on the Cross by José Risueño, whose replica is paraded in the procession on Wednesday of Holy Week. In the **sacristy**, which is decorated with some small paintings of the Italian school, there is an extremely beautiful chalice table made of inlaid marble, with patterns of arrows, cannons and indigenous motifs. This table, made in Peru in the 16th century, was a gift from the father of the archbishop of Castro, who was the Viceroy in that country.

The last place to visit are the **Sacred Caves**, which are outside the church. They were discovered accidentally in the 16th century. This is where the "leaden books" and the furnaces where they apparently burned the above-mentioned martyrs were found. This is also where the wooden cross St. John of God used when he was asking for alms is kept. There are several chapels: one dedicated to Our Lady of the Caves, another with an enormous stone (they say that any woman that kisses it will marry that year), and the last one, which is vaulted with different entrance arches, where there are four very beautiful small statues of St. Lucy, St. Teresa, St. Bruno and St. Francis, of the Risueño school.

Courtyard of the former Main Mosque of the Albaycin, now the Church of Salvador.

Upper Albaycin

Every street and corner affords us a different viewpoint for contemplating the Alhambra.

At the end of Cuesta del Chapiz we are already in the upper part of the quarter. This is where the most traditional and most typical Albaycin squares and streets are. Such are its features and peculiarity that sometimes you feel you are in a different town and not in Granada at all. There are three main squares that are a must to visit: **Plaza Larga**, **Plaza de San Nicolás** and **Plaza de San Miguel Bajo**. We will stop off at the most important monuments along the itinerary that links them all together. However, please note that many of them can only be visited at times of worship or they can only be seen inside on a guided visit.

The first one we come across in the open area that Cuesta del Chapiz ends up in is the **Church of Salvador** (Our Saviour), the main church in the quarter, since in Muslim times it was the "Main Mosque of the Albaycin", the second largest in Granada and the most beautiful of them all. It was converted into a parish church in 1501, although it

was later demolished to build another church, which was then burned down and destroyed in the Civil War. It was entirely rebuilt and the ornamental elements and altars it now has were brought from other churches a few years ago. However, the courtyard has managed to retain almost its original state. It is a typical lemon and orange tree courtyard that all mosques used to have, with a large cistern in the centre, surrounded by horseshoe arches. The columns the arches are resting on were replaced by stone buttresses.

A short distance away is the heart of the quarter and the meeting point of its people: **Plaza Larga**. Some of the bars and *tascas* with the most authentic Albaycin feel are in the streets surrounding this square. The **Puerta de las Pesas** (Gate of Weights) stands in one of its corners. It owes its name to the fact that the weights taken away from traders committing

fraud when measuring were hung up here. It dates from the 11th century, in the Zirid age, and it linked the Albaycin with the "Old Alcazaba" (fortress). The way to **Plaza de San Nicolás** is on the other side of the gate, taking the street on the left. This is a Square not to be missed when you come to Granada, since without any doubt whatsoever, it has the most universal and well-known view of

this city: Sierra Nevada, the Generalife, the Alhambra with its aligned towers and the entire city and vega (fertile plain) at our feet! The **Church of San Nicolás** (St. Nicholas) is in this square, built in 1525, on the site of a former mosque. It was one of the oldest and most beautiful churches in Granada, but unfortunately a deliberate fire was started during the uprisings in the years prior to the Civil War, on 10 August 1932, which destroyed the majority of it. Thankfully, those years of intolerance and fanaticism have long gone and the proof of that lies in the building next to it: the **Albaycin Mosque**, which opened for worship in 2003. After five centuries, the Koran is again being read in this place, and many of the prayers written on the walls of the Alhambra as a decoration come to life again in the voices of the people who come to pray here.

The next building to visit, which is also very near, is the **Convent of Santa Isabel la Real** (St. Isabella the Royal), founded in 1501 by Queen Isabella. First it was located in the Palace of Dar Al-Horra. Later it moved to the new convent, built on the same estate as the palace. The Church was built first. The **doorway** is by Enrique Egás, in Gothic Isabelline style, in the form of a Florentine arch, with the symbols of the Catholic Monarchs on its spandrels and their coat of arms in the central section. On the left is the

tower, built in 1549, where there are some lovely Moorish tiles in the top section. The **inside** of the church, which can be visited during hours of worship, is extremely beautiful. The most surprising are its ceilings: the one over the nave is made of wood in Mudéjar style, the one over the chancel is also made of wood, in a striking style that could be classified as "English Gothic". The **high altar retable**, at the top of a steep staircase, dates from the 16th century, with some alterations made in the 18th century. It is divided into two tiers and the crowning piece. The bottom section includes reliefs of the "Adoration of the Shepherds" and the "Circumcision", accompanied by statues of "St. Francis" and "St. Clare". The top section contains paintings of "St. John the Baptist" and "St. Elizabeth". There is a "Christ on the Cross" in the middle section, accompanied by small sculptures of Our Lady and St. John the Evangelist. At the very top, the crowning piece is a pediment with the figure of God the Father. The best part of the convent's interior is the **cloister**, dating from the last quarter of the 16th century, which can only be seen on a guided visit as it is in the secluded area. It is known as the "cloister of the Catholic Monarchs" and it has a beautiful courtyard with a fountain in the centre and a double arcade surrounding it, with seven arches on each side.

Directly opposite the Convent of Santa Isabel la Real, in Calle de la Tiña, is the **Hospital de la Tiña** (Ringworm Hospital) or **Casa del Marqués de Zenete**. This former house/palace of the Marquis of Zenete, dating from the 15th century, owes its name to the fact that it was a hospital for curing patients suffering from ringworm in the 17th

century. The most outstanding part that has survived to this day is its lovely recently restored courtyard. This is where Boabdil lived between September 1486 and April 1487, a time when there were internal conflicts in the royal Nasrid family and Granada had two kings: Boabdil in the Albaycin, and his uncle Zagal in the Alhambra.

Behind the Convent of Santa Isabel la Real, in Calle del Ladrón del Agua, is the **Palace of Dar Al-Horra**. Its name, which means "house of the honest queen", stems from the fact that Boabdil's mother lived in this palace when she was repudiated by her husband, King Muley Hacen, who married the Christian Isabel de Solís. It was part of the same estate belonging to the royal Nasrid family where the Convent of Santa Isabel la Real was built. The Catholic Monarchs did not demolish it, they respected it and added the convent to it. As mentioned above, it was the first house the nuns occupied before the new convent

The north side, which is the better preserved, has two storeys, with another arcade at the top and a lovely mirador on the bottom floor. This is the clearest example of the many Arab houses there were in the Albaycin, many of which still exist, which help us to imagine the grandeur and magnificence this quarter had in Moorish and Muslim times gone by.

The last square of the three mentioned above as the most important in this upper part of the Albaycin is the **Plaza de San Miguel Bajo**, almost connected with the Convent of Santa Isabel and the Palace of Dar Al-Horra. Surrounded by bars and terraces, it is an ideal place to relax and chat. The Church in the square, called **San Miguel** (St. Michael) was built to replace a mosque, as so many others were. It is so poorly decorated inside now that it is almost bare, since many of its works of art have gone to other churches.

In Calle San José, which is very close by, there is a church called **San José** (St. Joseph), the former

Top:
Detail of the main courtyard in Dar Al-Horra.

Bottom:
Merciful Christ, by José de Mora, in the Church of San José.

Right:
Chancel of the Church of San José.

was built. As in every Arab palace, the space is arranged around a beautiful courtyard with a small pool in the centre. There are two galleries with three arches each on the north and south sides.

"Jima de Al Morabitín", one of the oldest mosques in Muslim Granada. It was transformed into a parochial church in 1501 and later demolished and a new Christian church was built instead in 1525. All that is left of the old jima are the cistern and the minaret, dating from the 10th century. Inside, its most striking element is the chancel, with a Mudéjar coffered ceiling and a retable dating from the 12th century, designed by Ventura Rodríguez, which replaced an even earlier one. The image in the centre is "St. Joseph with Child", by Ruiz del Peral. Reliefs of the "Adoration of the Shepherds" and of the "Adoration of the Magi" are on either side, between columns. The top section, which dominates the whole, contains an image of a "Christ on the Cross". In the first chapel on the left of the high altar, the most interesting of the side chapels, there is an exceptional image, a "Christ on the Cross" by José de Mora, called "Cristo de la Misericordia" (Merciful Christ). The replica of this image is paraded in the Silent Procession on Thursday of Holy Week and, together with the "St. Bruno", by the same artist, or Alonso Cano's "Immaculate Conception", it has a place of honour in religious imagery in Granada. There are two very interesting small retables in the same chapel, one Renaissance style and the other Gothic.

There are two suggestions for the end of this itinerary of the Albaycin. First, you can go down **Calle San José** until you get to **Calle Calderería**, which in recent years has become more like a souk, full of teahouses and Moorish craftwork shops. Or second, you can go back to Plaza San Miguel and go to Puerta de Elvira via **Carril de la Lona** and **Cuesta de la Alhacaba**. As you go down, you will come across the restored **Monaita Gate**, on the right, half way down Carril de la Lona. This is another of the gates that were part of the ramparts of the Alcazaba (fortress) in the Zirid age. Its former name, which it was known by before the 17th century, was **Bibalbonaidar**, which means "Gate of the Ages". And right at the end of this descent there is another gate, the emblematic **Puerta de Elvira**, set in a large open space, the most important of all the gates and main entrance to the city in former times.

Top:
*Calle Calderería, a real souk, full of teahouses
and Moorish craftwork shops.*

Centre:
Monaita Gate, previously known as Bibalbonaidar.

Bottom:
Elvira Gate, the main entrance to the city in former times.

The Cathedral
and its surroundings

Map of the area

MONOGRAPHS INCLUDED

① CATHEDRAL, PAGE 128

② ROYAL CHAPEL, PAGE 152

③ CHURCH OF SAGRARIO, PAGE 170

⓸ MADRAZA, PAGE 172

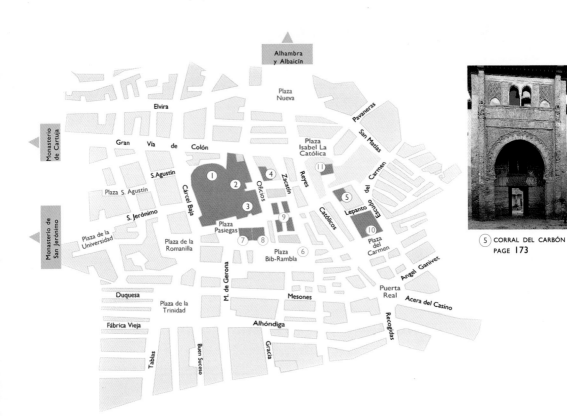

Alhambra y Albaicín

Monasterio de Cartuja

Monasterio de San Jerónimo

Plaza Nueva

Elvira

Pavaneras

Gran Vía de Colón

San Matías

Plaza Isabel La Católica

del Carmen

S.Agustín

Reyes

Zacatín

Plaza S. Agustín

Cárcel Baja

Oficios

① ⑪

② ④

S. Jerónimo

③ ⑤ Lepanto Escudo

Católicos

Plaza de la Universidad

Plaza Pasiegas

⑨

⑩

Plaza de la Romanilla

⑦ ⑧

Plaza del Carmen

Plaza Bib-Rambla ⑥

Ángel Ganivet

Duquesa

Puerta Real Acera del Casino

Plaza de la Trinidad

M. de Gerona

Mesones

Fábrica Vieja

Alhóndiga

Recogidas

Tablas

Buen Suceso

Gracia

⑤ CORRAL DEL CARBÓN PAGE 173

MAP OF THE AREA

USEFUL INFORMATION:

– The Cathedral (number 1) and the Royal Chapel (number 2) are the two most important monuments in this chapter and are well worth a visit.

INTRODUCTION
and itinerary

The historic centre and heart of Granada is one of the most emblematic places in the city, full of marvellous and interesting spots.

Top:
Monument in Plaza Isabel la Católica. It commemorates Columbus' meeting with Queen Isabella, who financed his voyage to America.

Right:
Calle Reyes Católicos, in the centre of the City.

The streets and squares found here are without a doubt the most important in Granada, as they form the real historic and commercial "centre" of the city. Since Islamic times, this has been an area of vital importance, where the most significant activities of its peoples have taken place in just a few metres. All this has shaped one of the most symbolic areas in Granada, due to both its monuments and urban landscape. The city's most emblematic buildings are here, as well as the two best known monuments after the Alhambra: **The Cathedral** and **The Royal Chapel**.

There are other extremely valuable and beautiful monuments, which travellers sometimes come across by chance, and which would merit an express visit in another city that does not have such a great wealth of monuments: **The Church of Sagrario** (Tabernacle), next to the Cathedral, located on the site where the Main Mosque in the city stood; **the Madraza**, the Arab University, where Theology and Law were studied. The City Hall was formerly located in its remodelled

Plaza Bibarrambla

building; and **the Corral del Carbón** (Coal Yard), a place of meeting and accommodation for the merchants of Muslim Granada. These three monuments will be described separately in this chapter in the section **"Other monuments of interest"**.

Other buildings in the centre worth visiting are: the **Palacio Arzobispal** (Archbishop's Palace), in the square called Plaza de Alonso Cano. Next to it is the **Palacio de la Curia Eclesiástica** (Ecclesiastical Curia Palace), one of the most interesting of Renaissance Granada, built as the headquarters of the University founded by Charles V in 1526. The Palace called the **Palacio de los Duques de Abrantes**, whose construction dates from the 16th century, with a Gothic style doorway and Mudéjar arches in the square called Plaza de Tovar. The **Ayuntamiento de Granada** (City Hall) in the square called Plaza del Carmen, located in part of the former Convento del Carmen (Carmelite Convent), dating from the 17th century.

The best part of this area in Granada is **Plaza Bibarrambla**, one of the most typical squares in the city. This is where the former Muslim metropolis ended. In those days, it was much smaller and hardly resembled the current square at all. It was the Plaza Mayor –the Main Square- in Granada, where all the city's ceremonies and fiestas were held. There was an extremely famous gate in the square, called "Orejas" (Ears) and in the 16th century "Manos" (Hands) because these parts of the bodies of executed people were hung there. It is totally unclear why this gate was removed from here and placed in the woods of the Alhambra, where it stands today. The square now has a special charm and it is one of the Granadines' favourite meeting places. Its traditional flower stalls and the terraces of its bars and restaurants not only enhance the square, but also make it a lively place to be, especially in the spring and summer months. The "Fountain of Neptune or of the Giants", dating from the 17th century, is in the centre, although it was placed here at a later date.

Next to this square is the **Alcaiceria**, a secluded reminder of the old Muslim city. The part that is still standing today is a partial reconstruction of what this Muslim trading quarter was once like. Founded in the 14th century by Yusuf I, its main activity was silk trading, although other traders set up business here too. Its name comes from the Arab word "al-Qaysaryya", meaning "Caesar's House", which, according to the historian Hurtado de Mendoza, was the name given to this type of market in the Arab world as a token of gratitude towards Emperor Justin I (518-527), who granted the Scenite Arabs the privilege of producing and selling silk.

The small part we can see today is a reconstruction, but it gives us an idea of what it must have been like. It stretched from Plaza Bibarrambla almost to Plaza Nueva, and from what is today the street called Calle Reyes Católicos to the Mosque, which is now the Church of Sagrario. Unfortunately, the Alcaiceria burned down on the night of

Detail of the outside of the Royal Chapel.

Detail of the Doorway of Curia Palace.

Detail of the Facade of the Corral del Carbón.

20 July 1843 and the minimal area still left helps us to appreciate on a small scale what it once was: a myriad of narrow streets and small squares with almost two hundred shops. There were ten access gates, which were closed at night and watched over by guards with dogs. The houses were only one storey high and not very deep. The best known was the house of the "Gelices", which was next to the Mosque. This is where the offices of the "gelices", or silk trade lessors, were. There was also a Customs House and a silk administration building.

Apart from the silk market, which was the most important, there were others for woollen cloth, wool, clothes and many other things. Every street was named after the business carried out there. The "Zacatín" was the main street running through the quarter. Its name comes from "al-Saqqatin", which means "sellers of cheap goods" or "used clothes dealers", but there were also silversmiths, haberdashers and esparto craftsmen. This street still exists, but it is totally different from the one that completely disappeared in the fire. The name of another one of its streets is curious. It is called "Hombres de Confianza", which means Trustworthy Men, and it may have been slightly

ironical given that this was the location of the money changers and lenders, who were probably Jews, since the Koran forbade Muslims to engage in this practice.

After the conquest, this quarter was included under the jurisdiction of the Alhambra, and was ruled by the Governor of the latter. In 1501 a Royal Warrant proclaimed that silk could only be traded in Spain in the alcaicerias in Malaga, Granada and Almeria, as in Muslim times. In the Alcaiceria standing today, which has three streets and one small square, a series of Granadine traders have established their businesses, selling craftwork and souvenirs, in the manner of the former Muslim merchants.

The Cathedral

Devised by the Catholic Monarchs as a symbol of the expansion of Christianity, the one who was the real driving force behind the construction was Charles V.

The Cathedral is an example of the purest Renaissance art, but as a result of the extremely long construction period, it is a mixture of Gothic, Renaissance, Baroque and Neoclassicism. However, the majority is Renaissance style.

Although the actual building of the Cathedral was not started until 1523, the Catholic Monarchs had decided to have the work done a long time before, in 1501. The Main Mosque, the former cathedral see, had become too small, so the Monarchs made the decision to build a new temple as the see, much more in tune with the importance Granada should have as the symbol of the expansion of Christianity. With this in mind, they made a donation of all the Main Mosque's possessions, income and stipends for the future Cathedral. They also gave the Monstrance used for the Corpus Christi procession, crosses and other belongings. However, as the Catholic Monarchs were more interested in completing the Royal Chapel (which was to be the Monarchs' memorial chapel so that they could be laid to rest in Granada) they postponed the building of the Cathedral. The Royal Chapel was finished, or at least its first phase was completed, in 1515, a year before King Ferdinand died. The actual building

Left: *Main facade of the Cathedral. It was designed by Alonso Cano.*

Top: *Detail of the apse, seen from Calle Gran Vía.*

129

of the Cathedral was not started until some years later and the one who was actually the real driving force behind the construction was Charles V.

Master Enrique Egas was responsible for the Gothic style design in 1518. The first stone was laid on 25 March 1523, on the day of Incarnation, which the temple is dedicated to. The plague postponed the work, which was resumed in 1524. Enrique Egas worked on the building from then on until 1528, when he was dismissed and replaced by Diego de Siloé. The latter's greatest achievement was adapting Egas' Gothic design to a construction more in line with the times of the day: Roman style. In 1561, although still unfinished (the chevet was barely covered), it was prepared for worship. Siloé died in 1563 and he was succeeded by Juan de Maeda. But the revolution of the Moriscos in 1568 caused the works to be cancelled. From then on, different master architects succeeded each other as project managers, among others, Alonso Cano, who designed the facade, which was very different to the one Siloé had initially outlined. The building was finally completed in 1704, over one hundred and eighty years after the first stone had been laid.

THE EXTERIOR FACADES

The **main facade**, which is on the *west side*, was designed by Alonso Cano in 1667, not long before he died. It has a framework of three large doorways resembling three large triumphal arches. The medallion in relief above the door in the centre represents the Incarnation, the name of the church, with a cartouche in relief of "Ave Maria", the work of such a magnificent sculptor as Risueño. The two figures on either side of this door are the apostles Peter and Paul and they are attributed to Duque Cornejo. There are two reliefs in the recesses crowning the side doors representing the Assumption of Mary and the Visitation, which are the work of Miguel and Luis Pedro Verdiguier. They were also responsible for the medallions with the evangelists, appearing below the central cornice, and the images above it, representing the Old and the New Testament and the Archangels Michael and Raphael.

Worth mentioning on the *north side* facade is the **Door of St. Jerome**, which is located past the tower, and above all, the **Door of Forgiveness**. The first part of this door, by Diego de Siloé, is perhaps the most important sculpture work by this artist. It has two Corinthian columns on either side. There are two allegorical figures of "Faith" and "Justice" on the spandrels above the semicircular arch. They are holding a cartouche in Latin where it states that Faith and Justice gave the city to the Catholic Monarchs and the see to its first archbishop, Brother Hernando de Talavera. The second part is by Ambrosio de Vico, and it is crowned by the figure of God the Father (inside the arch).

The only thing worth mentioning on the *east side* is the **Door of Ecce Homo**, the cathedral's oldest door, which Siloé designed and Sancho del Cerro constructed. This is the end of the outside itinerary, since the Cathedral does not have a *south* facade, as it is right next to the **Church of Sagrario** and the **Royal Chapel** on this side.

Top:
Detail of the medallion above the main door. It represents the Incarnation.

Right:
Door of Forgiveness, on the north side.

The Cathedral was actually meant to have had twin towers, but as there were plans to build the Church of Sagrario (Tabernacle) on one side of it, the idea was rejected. There is only one tower, which has three sections, with a total height of about fifty metres, and it is not finished. Siloé's project was with two towers, each with a height of eighty metres. In this initial project the three sections were cube shaped, as the tower is now, and there was a fourth octagon shaped section. However, as the tower was weakened in 1590, the fourth section was never added. Later, in 1636, they made another attempt to add it, but it did not work out, so it was therefore left unfinished. The current tower is square and it can be seen from any high part of Granada and its magnificence is a symbol of the city.

INSIDE PLAN AND ELEVATION

Once inside it is hard not to be amazed by the grandness of the nave, aisles and columns and how very white it is, giving the impression of being more like a Renaissance palace than a cathedral. It is not a church calling us to prayer and meditation, but rather to amazement and exaltation of the human spirit. It is here that the Granadine Cathedral both surprises us and fills us with admiration.

There are two very different sections in the cathedral, which are described below:

a) The Gothic plan, designed by Enrique Egas, just like Toledo Cathedral, with an ambulatory. The Latin cross gets totally lost in its surroundings with the chapels around the ambulatory connected at the buttresses, forming

niches, so that attention is not distracted from the High Altar.

b) The elevation of the columns and the Chancel, which changes the primitive Gothic idea and transforms it into a Renaissance temple with Roman design. Siloé's trip to Italy was not in vain, as he took advantage of it to be inspired by columns with Corinthian capitals and the adaptation of cubic and cylindrical elements for his design of the Chancel (this had already been seen in Florence with the work of Brunelleschi and with Bramante and Michelangelo in St. Peter's in Rome). Siloé made the rectangular plan con-

PLAN OF THE CATHEDRAL
(The Church of Sagrario [Tabernacle] and the Royal Chapel are shown as annexes)

CHURCH OF SAGRARIO
It takes up a large part of the site where the former Main Mosque was located. It was built a long time after the Cathedral.

ROYAL CHAPEL
Originally designed as a chapel belonging to the Cathedral, it was built before the latter. It kept its independence and that of the institutions governing it.

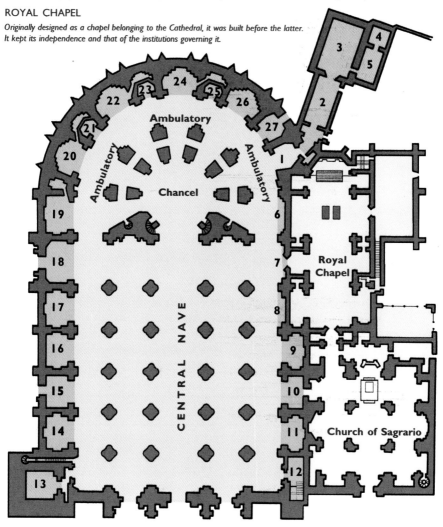

CATHEDRAL

1. Sacristy Doorway
2. Sacristy Anteroom
3. Sacristy
4. Chapter House Oratory
5. Chapter House
6. Retable of St. James
7. Royal Chapel Doorway
8. Jesus of Nazareth Retable
9. Chapel of the Holy Trinity
10. Sagrario Door
11. Chapel of St. Michael
12. Accounts Department Door
13. Doorway of the former Chapter House (now a museum)
14. Chapel of Our Lady of the Pillar
15. Door of St. Jerome
16. Chapel of Our Lady of Mount Carmel
17. Chapel of Our Lady of Sorrows
18. Door of Forgiveness
19. Chapel of Our Lady of Antigua
20. Chapel of St. Lucy
21. Chapel of the Suffering Christ
22. Chapel of St. Teresa
23. Chapel of St. Blaise
24. Chapel of St. Cecilius
25. Chapel of St. Sebastian
26. Chapel of St. Anne
27. Door of Ecce Homo

verge towards the circle of the Chancel, the focus of our attention. The Chancel, with its vault rising to an enormous height, is the centre of all the axes radiating from the main door and from the ambulatory. There are no significant side chapels or choir to distract our attention. This is where this cathedral's enormous value lies, in the fact that Siloé was able to use what Egas had left and adapt it to a totally new idea, making the most of the rectangular arm of the crossing, which would have divided the Cathedral into two well-defined sectors.

THE CENTRAL NAVE

We should stop for a moment to admire the grandness and perfection of the shapes of the central nave, which immediately reminds us of the large Italian temples of the time, despite being smaller. It would not even be sinful to compare it with St. Peter's at the Vatican, albeit on a much smaller scale. The cross-ribbed vaults with different motifs are an innovation within Renaissance art. The width of the nave and columns, as well as the relatively low height of the vaults and cross-ribs, lead us to believe that Siloé made an allowance for earthquakes when he planned the elevation of the cathedral.

The lack of a choir in the centre, which would decrease visibility and grandness, is worth emphasising. The correct decision was made to remove the choir in 1926 and transfer it back to its original position, behind the Chancel.
The contrast of lights, whiteness, stained glass windows and the design of the twin organs (in the centre of the nave) lend it a quality unsurpassed in any other Spanish church. The columns do not stand individually but in blocks of four, and their base not only enhances them, but also makes them even higher. We could say that it is from here where you can admire Siloé's and Cano's work to the full. The entire expanse of the cathedral can also be admired. It is one hundred and fifteen metres long by sixty-seven wide.

Previous page:
The Cathedral from its central nave.
The Chancel is in the background.

Bottom:
The ceiling from the centre of the nave.

Right in the centre of the nave is the "Vault of the Archbishops", the place where the famous Alonso Cano was laid to rest. However, this was not known until very recently, which means that he was not buried in a preferential site, as he should have been.

The **twin organs** deserve a special mention. They are at the end of the sides of the central

nave and are a product of the 18th century, when organ music was at its peak. They were completed in 1745 and 1749 and especially placed in that location to mark the end of the choir, which was there at the time. Their creator is Leonardo Fernández Dávila, and it is immediately obvious that they are Spanish, because the trumpets are in a fan shape, pointing outwards like batteries of cannons, in contrast to the central European organ, which only has vertical pipes.

THE CHANCEL

Sit down in the centre of the nave and take a look at the framework. The Chancel is located behind a triumphal arch, which is covered with a chancel arch, which gets narrower as it reaches the centre. The wall decoration is based on the stained glass windows of the two storeys above and on the paintings by Alonso Cano portraying the Virgin Mary's life.

The vault is forty-five metres high and the diameter of the base is twenty-two metres. It was completely decorated by Siloé and has stained glass windows, the work of Teodoro de Holanda and Jan van Campen, between 1554 and 1561. Their motifs are the Life and Passion of Jesus Christ and Biblical scenes.

Immediately below are the seven large paintings by Alonso Cano, which he used to fill the spaces (probably originally for more windows), commissioned by the Chapter, to honour the Virgin Mary, to whom this cathedral is dedicated, in particular to the Mystery of the Incarnation.

The seven paintings (only three are seen head on) represent Mary from her birth to Assumption. Cano was faced with a huge problem, as the enormous height and size of the spaces made the

Top:
Detail of the silver baldachin in the centre of the high altar, with the cupola enclosing the Chancel in the background.

project difficult, since the figures could have ended up being too elongated, or too small if he had divided the pictures into two halves. Another problem was the colours, which had to be bright and cheerful, but not strident, so that they were not overshadowed by the light of the stained glass windows.

Cano solved these problems in an original manner: the figures were raised on steps or parapets at the bottom, or the top section was filled with heavenly scenes or architectural scenery, so the figures were a normal size. The colours are brilliant, but as they are "framed" in gold, they are highlighted and are not affected by the light from the stained glass windows. The painting in the middle of the seven, depicting "The Incarnation", has a well-known detail, which is the fact that the Archangel Gabriel is kneeling with his wings pointing to the ground, showing reverence towards the Virgin Mary and extolling her.

The bottom section is decorated with paintings of the Doctors of the Church. Their names are written in Latin and they cover the niches that were originally going to be for the tombs of monarchs, which was what Charles V had planned, as he wanted to have a Royal Vault here, and then for archbishops. But they were never used. Philip II later decided that the *Monastery of El Escorial* would be the vault where the mortal remains of Spanish Monarchs would rest. The paintings are by Bocanegra and Juan de Sevilla. Immediately below them are gilded statues of the twelve apostles, which were created by Martín de Aranda, Bernabé de Gavira and Alonso de Mena.

The praying statues of the Catholic Monarchs, by Pedro de Mena, are on either side and above them are the busts of Adam and Eve, the work of Cano, which have a Michelangelo touch, especially the way their heads are turned.

Further on you come across two Baroque pulpits, one on either side, made of marble from Lanjarón (a town in the Alpujarras of Granada). They are the work of Francisco Hurtado Izquierdo, in the same style as the retable of Nuestra Señora de las Angustias (Our Lady of Sorrows). The candelabras were designed by Cano and made by the silversmith Diego Cervantes Pacheco.

All that is left to see is the high altar, in the form of a baldachin, which is modern, the work of José Navajas Parejo, and placed in 1926. It is made of sliver, with a base of serpentine, which comes from the Sierra Nevada, which José Navajas Parejo was also responsible for. It was paid for by the Duke of San Pedro Galatino (a great patron of Granada, whose remains are lying in the *Chapel of Our Lady of Antigua* in this cathedral). Behind it is the choir, dating from the 16th century. Between the altar and the choir there is the lectern, the work of Cano and made of serpentine and mahogany with gilded bronze decorations.

Right:
Details of the two Baroque pulpits, on either side of the high altar.
They are the work of Francisco Hurtado Izquierdo.

Alonso Cano
"The Spanish Michelangelo"
(1601-1667)

He was born in Granada, the son of Miguel Cano and María de Almansa. His father was a woodcarver who worked on several retables and Cano therefore got his interest in them from him. His father decided to move to Seville, where there was more artistic activity, in 1614, apparently because of a commission or the lack of renowned artists. Cano was 13 years old at the time.

In Seville he joined Francisco Pacheco's studio in 1616 to both study and work. This was where he later met the universal genius of painting, Diego Velázquez, and they became good friends. Cano worked in this studio for five years, learning the art of painting. He learnt the art of architecture, as well as retable designing, from his father and the art of sculpture from Martínez Montañes, also in Seville. All these influences turned Cano into a complete and brilliant artist. While he was in Seville he was responsible for important works of art, such as the "Retable of the Church of Lebrija" and the "Painting of St. Francis Borgia".

As far as his private life is concerned, he married María de Figuerda in 1625, but was widowed two years later when she died in childbirth. Saddened by his widowerhood, he later married a girl who was about twelve years old in 1631. Her name was María Magdalena de Uceda, who came with a large dowry and a black slave. But Cano, in spite of the vast sums he earned from his commissions, as well as his wife's dowry, ended up in the debtor's jail as a result of his bad administration and excessive expenditure, above all on books, houses and works of art.

In 1638 he went to Madrid for the first time at the age of 37, with an extraordinary

Previous page:
"The Visitation" (1563). One of the seven paintings by Alonso Cano decorating the Chancel.

Top:
Portrait of Alonso Cano.
(Image supplied by the Fine Arts Museum in Cadiz).

training in the three above-mentioned plastic arts behind him. When he arrived in Madrid, his old friend Velázquez and Juan de Pareja acted as his patrons. Velázquez also interceded with the Count-Duke of Olivares so that he could enter the Court of Philip IV as a painter and valet. He was also appointed drawing teacher of Prince Baltasar Carlos, the son of Philip IV. Only one work has been acknowledged as his during his time in Madrid: "The Miracle at the Well", since the majority of his artistic activity consisted in restoring paintings, in spite of the fact that he was not very interested in working then and spent a great deal of time studying paintings and drawings.

In 1644 an unfortunate event was to disrupt his life for ever: the murder of his second wife, who was stabbed repeatedly, apparently by a young man Cano had allowed to study in his studio. The master was accused of murdering her and was therefore tortured by the Inquisition, with their "usual" methods. Nevertheless, his torturers did not touch either his right arm or hand, which may have been out of respect for his mastery, or perhaps because the King interceded for him. Thankfully, Cano survived that terrible process unscathed and innocent.

Embittered, lonely and resentful, he moved to Valencia that same year, with the idea of entering the Monastery of "Porta Coeli" as a Carthusian. He was so convinced that this was what he was going to do that he left all his personal property there. In the end, he gave up on the idea and for a few years he lived a bad-tempered and quarrelsome life that even got him involved in some duels. In 1651 he turned his life around again, when once more he decided on a religious life and requested entry as a canon into the

Cathedral of Granada, the city where he had been born. As the only place vacant in 1652 was that of a musician, he was offered the position of "prebendary[1]". However, instead of giving his part or prebend as a musician or singer, he did it with paintings, sculptures and architecture, which embellished the Cathedral, as it still had many spaces to fill and part of the building had not been finished, such as the vaults and the main facade.

To enter into the cathedral body he had to pass the blood purity test. This meant proving that he did not have any Jewish ancestors, so he naturally passed without any problems. What is more, Cano felt an enormous hostility towards Jews, which became obsessive. It disgusted him when they touched his clothes and he did not walk where they had gone before. Once even, when he was very ill, the parish priest from the Church of Santiago (St. James) went to administer the Eucharist to him. Cano very serenely asked him if he also gave the sacraments to repentant Jews. When he replied that he did, Cano said: "Go with God... because he who gives the sacraments to Jews is not going to give them to me", and he dismissed him and had the priest from the Church of San Andrés (St. Andrew) called instead.

In his position as a prebendary, the canons provided him with a home and a studio on the first floor of the tower. He was even exempted from attending religious services when he was creating works of art for the Cathedral, except on Sundays and public holidays. Nevertheless, his relations with the canons cannot have been very good, since they complained that he did no work of any importance and even went as far as questioning his ability as a painter. The master, in the face of the chapter's doubts about his artistic abilities, as well as their stinginess over paying him his stipends and work materials (at one time

Left:
"The Assumption" (Alonso Cano, 1662-1663).
It decorates the Chancel.

[1] A prebendary is a person who contributes his part or prebend to a cathedral or collegiate church. In this case, he had to contribute the "prebend" of his voice to the choir.

they went for four years without paying him) started not to attend the services and annoy them as much as possible. These differences led to his ordination as a clergyman being postponed and Cano leaving for Madrid again in 1657.

It is quite curious that the chapter thought the work Cano had done when he was first in Granada was "not much", since the master had completed the following works, among others: he designed the high altar's two silver lamps, he did the lectern, he planned the seven paintings on the life of the Virgin Mary for the high altar, he designed the plans for the Church and Convent of "Angel Custodio" (where the "Bank of Spain" is today), he painted fourteen paintings, he made the famous sculptures of saints (in wood), which are now in the Fine Arts Museum in Granada and, above all, his great sculpted work, one of the most important Spanish sculptures of all time "The Immaculate Conception" (1655-56), which was initially planned for the top of the lectern[2].

Once in Madrid, he obtained permission from the king to be ordained as a clergyman, and this finally happened in Salamanca in March 1658. With this prebend and with the support of Philip IV, he was readmitted into Granada as a prebendary in 1660. In addition, the canons, who had been so miserly before, ended up paying him everything they owed.

However, in this last period of his life, Cano was not well treated by the cathedral chapter. For when he had finished the seven paintings of "The Life of the Virgin Mary" (which embellish the High Altar), as well as "Our Lady of Bethlehem" (planned for the lectern, instead of "The Immaculate Conception"), the canons took his home in the tower away from him, ordering him to leave immediately. They really did not know how to thank him for his work, even though the chapter thought that the two sculptures of the Virgin Mary made for the lectern ("The Immaculate Conception" and "Our Lady of Bethlehem") were so beautiful that they preferred to change their initial location for another where they could be admired better and more closely.

Perhaps an anecdote from this time of Cano's life will make it easier to understand this brilliant artist's strength of character. In 1666, Cano made

Top:
"The Purification of the Blessed Virgin Mary and Presentation of the Child Jesus"
(Alonso Cano, 1655-1656).
It decorates the Chancel.

a small image of St. Anthony of Padua, which he had been commissioned by an *"oidor[3]"*. When the image was finished, the *oidor* asked him what the price was. The master replied that it was a hundred doubloons. As the *oidor* thought that the price was too high for the number of days worked, he told the artist that he was charging him almost a doubloon per day of work and that he, as "an *oidor* of Granada with more noble responsibility" did not earn that much. Cano, already rather angry, replied: "The king can make *oidores* from the dust of the earth, but only God can make an Alonso Cano" and full of rage, without waiting for an answer, he threw the figure onto the floor smashing it into smithereens.

[2] The lectern is extremely large and was used for choir books.
[3] A magistrate responsible for administering justice in the kingdom.

On the other hand, he was very charitable with the poor and helped them as much as he could. As he was always short of money, his alms consisted of doing a drawing for them, telling them afterwards who would buy it off them and how much they should be paid for it. This facet demonstrates his humility and kindness with the needy and his arrogance and quick temper with those who doubted his worth, whether they were noblemen, *oidores* or ministers of the Holy Church!

On 4 May 1667, the canons appointed him "Master Builder" of the cathedral. His last project, the cathedral's facade, was also approved that year, but Cano never saw it realised, as he died three months later. Possibly dating from this last period are the busts of "Adam" and "Eve", "St. Paul's Head", "The Immaculate Conception" in the cathedral's oratory, and "Jesus Meets his Mother on the Way to Calvary" or the "Via Dolorosa" of the

Jesus of Nazareth retable. He also did the design for the "Church of Magdalena" (Mary Magdalene) and the painting "Our Lady of the Rosary" in Malaga Cathedral.

Cano died on 3 September 1667. The canons' notice of his death and funeral, which was held quickly on the same day he died, was simple and very brief. At least they granted him the grace of being buried in the cathedral's crypt, as he had requested. And at the time of his death, we come across another anecdote of his life, demonstrating his character and sensitivity towards classic beauty. As he was dying, a priest came to see him with a crucifix on which the image sculpted "had not been very well done". When Cano saw it, he asked him to remove it from him. The priest answered: "My son, but why? The Lord redeemed you". To which Cano replied: "Father, do you want me to be irritated and get taken away by the devil? Give me a simple cross, I can worship and revere Him there and imagine Him with my own idea." And taking a basic wooden cross in his hands, he died.

He was so poor at the end of his days that he was not even able to leave a doubloon to pay for them to say masses for his soul. The little he had was in Valencia, at the Monastery of "Porta Coeli" already mentioned, and it amounted to some books, some illustrations and some moulds.

Cano was misunderstood, as he was born before his time. He was a Renaissance man in everything he did, as like them he was a master of all the plastic arts.

Left:
"The Incarnation" (Alonso Cano, 1652).
Of the seven paintings decorating the Chancel, this is the one in the centre, as this church is dedicated to the Mystery of the Incarnation.

Top left:
*Christ on the Cross
by Martínez Montañés.*

Top right:
General view of the Sacristy.

Bottom:
*The Immaculate Conception,
Cano's masterpiece.*

THE SACRISTY

Before entering, take a look at the beautiful doorway, by Diego de Siloé. This is a richly decorated door where a Madonna and Child stand out above the cornice. The figures of St. Peter and St. Paul are on either side. The heads of apostles and saints are carved on the panels of the door's magnificent walnut leaves.

The sacristy is at the end of a small passageway or ante-sacristy where the walnut wardrobes are, made for storing the priests' vestments. The only paintings worth mentioning in this anteroom are: "The Annunciation to the Shepherds", by Bassano, and one of the "Holy Family", by J. de Sevilla. In the Sacristy, dating from the 18th century, there is a "Christ on the Cross" by Martínez Montañés, of the Sevillian school, which dominates the room. Above it there is an "Annunciation" by A. Cano and under them, the masterpiece by the same man: "The Immaculate Conception", a small sculpture about 50 cm high, made of cedar. The silver base is later. It is, without a doubt, the best work in the Cathedral and perhaps, due to its beauty, its colours, her hands and its small size, the best sculpture to emerge from the Spanish 17th century.

Left:
*Retable of St. James
by Francisco Hurtado Izquierdo.
The image in the centre,
which gives the retable its name,
is the Apostle James or "Moor Slayer",
the work of Alonso de Mena.*

THE CHAPELS IN THE AISLES AND THE AMBULATORY

There now follows a description of the chapels and some of the doorways in the aisles and the ambulatory. The majority of the chapels date from the Baroque age and some are Neoclassical. However, as there are many of them, we will only give a brief summary of every one of them here and a more detailed description of those that are more interesting in our opinion. The itinerary starts with the first chapel on leaving the sacristy on the left, until the main door is reached, and in the aisle on the opposite side, from this door to the end of the ambulatory. There is a number next to every chapel or door indicating its location on the general plan on page 133.

Retablo de Santiago (6): This is Baroque style made of polychrome wood by Francisco Hurtado Izquierdo. The image in the centre represents the Apostle James or "Moor Slayer" (this is how he was known by the masses, since, according to tradition, he appeared in the battle of Clavijo in 857 and defeated them) and gives the retable its name. It is the work of Alonso de Mena. The side statues, by José and Diego Mora, represent St. Gregory and the patron of Granada, St. Cecilius. Above there is a small painting representing "Our Lady of Forgiveness", a present

The room is surrounded by a set of commodes, made of mahogany, designed by Miguel Verdiguier and made by Dezelles. There are some magnificent Baroque style dressing mirrors, from the Royal Mirror Factory in Paris, at the top of the commodes. Above them there is an "Apostolate" (a set of paintings of the Holy Apostles), by the School of José de Ribera, "El Españoleto", although the St. Peter may well be his.

Magdalene" and "St. Paul the Hermit", all by José Ribera (El Españoleto), although the last one mentioned (St. Paul) could be a copy. There are two portraits of "Jesus and Mary", as well as a "Jesus Meets Mary on the Way to Calvary" and a "St. Augustine", all by Alonso Cano. Lastly, there is a "St. Francis of Asis", attributed to El Greco because of its elongated design.

Capilla de la Santísima Trinidad (9): All that needs to be said about this chapel is that it owes its name to the painting at the top of the triptych, representing "the Mystery of the Holy Trinity". It is the work of Alonso Cano, a sketch of a larger one, which he

from Pope Innocent VIII to Queen Isabella. This painting presided over the altar, before which the first mass was held in Granada in the Alhambra, after the Reconquest. At the top, in the centre, there is a Virgin Mary (it may be by Risueño or by Mena) and on either side there are two paintings of the bishops St. Thomas of Villanova and St. Peter Paschal, by Risueño.

Portada de la Capilla Real (7): This doorway originally opened up onto the street, but when the Cathedral was built, right next to the Royal Chapel, it became an internal door. The design is by Enrique Egas, in Isabelline Gothic style. At the top of the door there is an Epiphany with the Madonna and Child, and St. George and St. James are on either side. The Catholic Monarchs' coat of arms and emblems can be seen above the door arch.

Retablo del Nazareno (8): This Baroque style Jesus of Nazareth retable, by Marcos Fernández Raya, was designed for framing paintings, which include, among others: "Baby Jesus Appearing to St. Anthony" (the highest and largest of them all), "Martyrdom of St. Lawrence", "Head of St. Peter", "Mary

painted for the Monastery of San Antón (St. Anthony). The latter is legendary, as they say that Cano painted it for the monks in the monastery in exchange for a dish of *"chanfainas"* (a type of lung stew).

Puerta del Sagrario (10): This door connects the Cathedral with the Church of Sagrario (Tabernacle). It is not very noteworthy, except for the "Annunciation" by Pedro Atanasio Bocanegra and a painting of "Jesus of Nazareth" on its right, which St. John of God prayed in front of. Opposite there is a copy of the miraculous "Christ of the Cloth", from the town of Moclín.

Capilla de San Miguel (11): This is the last chapel in this aisle and one of the last retables created (1804-1807). It is made of marble and is Neoclassical in style. The most interesting is the relief of "Archangel St. Michael", which lends its name to the chapel, carved in white marble by Juan Adán.

Puerta de la Contaduría (12): The last doorway in this aisle got its name from the offices of the Contaduría (Accounts Department) behind it. This was where the Cathedral's accounts and wealth were administered.

Portada de la antigua Sala Capitular (now a museum) (13): This is the first door you come across in the opposite aisle. It is by Maeda, a disciple of Siloé. The figures above the arch represent "Prudence" and "Justice". In a second section above the cornice there is a "Charity", by Diego Pesquera. The inside is the space of the tower. Formerly it was the cathedral's chapter house and it is now a small **museum** containing sculptures by Alonso Cano and Pedro de Mena, tapestries from Brussels, vestments embroidered by Moriscos in the 16th century, a Monstrance donated by Queen Isabella the Catholic for the Corpus Christi procession, chalices and different pieces of jewellery (donations by archbishops, monarchs and popes). Also worth noting is the painting of "The Madonna and Child", attributed to Leonardo Da Vinci.

Capilla de la Virgen del Pilar (14): This Neoclassical style chapel dedicated to Our Lady of the Pillar is made of marble and bronze. Its central retable represents the appearance of the Virgin Mary to St. James and it is by Juan Adán, who was also responsible for the other sculptures in the chapel. Next to this chapel is the **Puerta de San Jerónimo (St. Jerome) (15).** Its space was closed in to make a Room for Incumbents. At the moment it is a chapel, but it is not very interesting.

Capilla de la Virgen del Carmen (16): A late Baroque, almost Rococo style retable with an image of "Our Lady of Mount Carmel", who this chapel is dedicated to, in the centre, attributed to José de Mora. The

Left:
"Christ washing the Feet of his Disciples", "The Last Supper" and "The Agony in the Garden" (Teodoro de Holanda, 1559-1560).
These stained glass windows decorate the Chancel.

"The Crucifixion" (Jan van Campen, 1558-1561). Chancel of the Cathedral.

and "St. Thomas of Villanova". Also note the medallion in the upper section, representing "Veronica's Veil". After this retable and the crossing you come to the **Puerta del Perdón (Door of Forgiveness) (18)**.

Capilla de Nuestra Señora de la Antigua (19): This is another of the most interesting retables. It is Baroque, but with exaggerated decoration in the exuberant Churrigueresque[4] style. It is all made of polychrome wood with gold leaf. It was designed by Duque Cornejo. In the centre there is an image of "Our Lady of Antigua", which clashes with the overdecorated retable as it is simple and elegant (German Gothic style dating from the 15th century). This image of the Virgin Mary was a special devotion for the Catholic Monarchs, who brought it to Granada during the conquest and donated it to the Cathedral. The figures on either side of the Virgin Mary are "St. Gregory" and "St. Cecilius". Small paintings and reliefs with scenes of the life of the Virgin Mary and Jesus also decorate the retable. Crowning the

Top left:
Chapel of Our Lady of Sorrows.

Bottom:
Image in white marble
of Our Lady of Sorrows.

figures accompanying the Virgin Mary on either side are "St. Simon Stock" and "St. Elias". The lower section of the retable is taken up by an image of "St. Casilda Dead", by Torcuato Ruíz del Peral.

Capilla de la Virgen de las Angustias (17): This is perhaps the strangest and most original retable of them all, and it is also one of the most beautiful. It is made entirely of marble from Lanjarón, at the height of Andalusian Baroque. It is the work of José de Bada and the sculptures are by Agustín Vera Moreno. The most outstanding characteristic of this altar lies in the fact that there are no external elements supporting it, such as stone, wood or bronze.

There is a white marble image of "Nuestra Señora de las Angustias" (Our Lady of Sorrows), the patron of Granada, in the centre. The figures in the side niches, made of while marble and gilded, are the bishop saints: "St. Gregory", "St. Peter Paschal", "St. Nicholas of Bari"

[4] An ornamentation style with exaggerated decoration used by the Baroque architect and sculptor José de Churriguera at the end of the 17th century, who was widely imitated in Spanish architecture in the 18th century.

entire piece at the very top is the Archangel St. Michael, and the Archangels St. Raphael and St. Gabriel are at the sides.

Two portraits of the Catholic Monarchs praying, by Francisco Alonso Argüello, are on either side of the altar, sheltered by arches.

The Chapels of the Ambulatory: It is called the ambulatory because this is where pilgrims walked and slept in Roman churches. It is semicircular and it has the special feature of the High Altar being visible from anywhere in it, so that all the faithful staying there could follow the mass. It also houses an important **collection of choir books**, dating from the time of the Catholic Monarchs, and a collection of twenty-two stained glass windows made in the 16th century. The altars or chapels in the ambulatory are the following: **Santa Lucía (20)**, with retables by Gaspar Guerrero, and an image of St. Lucy in the centre; **Cristo de las Penas (Suffering Christ) (21)**, which gets its name from the "Stations of the Cross" dominating it, dating from the 16th century; **Santa Teresa (22)**, which also has a retable by Gaspar Guerrero, dedicated to St. Teresa, whose image

is in the centre; **San Blas (23)**, dominated by a sculpture of St. Blaise, who the chapel is named after, apparently from Alonso de Mena's studio, **San Cecilio (24)**, dedicated to the patron saint of Granada (St. Cecilius), in a Neoclassical style, with three white marble retables; **San Sebastián (25)**, whose name comes from the title of a painting of the martyrdom of St. Sebastian, by Juan de Sevilla; **Santa Ana (26)**, whose most significant element is a sculpture of "St. Anne, the Madonna and Child", a work by Diego Pesquera, with paintings representing the life of the Virgin Mary painted by Pedro de Raxis. The space immediately after this last chapel is the door called **Puerta del Ecce Homo (27)**, which completes the itinerary.

The Royal Chapel

*The Catholic Monarchs ordered
a chapel to be built in Granada
so that their mortal remains could
be buried there. Another indication
of their love for this city and
of the importance it would
have in the new age.*

The Catholic Monarchs, Ferdinand II of Aragon and Isabella I of Castile, ordered a Chapel to be built by a Royal Warrant dated 13 September 1504, to be dedicated to St. John the Baptist and St. John the Evangelist, next to the Chancel of the Cathedral in Granada, so that their mortal remains could be buried there. However, Queen Isabella died that very year in Medina del Campo, so King Ferdinand continued to manage the project until his death in 1516.

The first part of the work, which was the construction of the building in a Gothic style (1505-1517) was done almost entirely by King Ferdinand. After the king's death, the Catholic Monarchs' grandson, Charles I (1517-1556), better known as Charles V, took over. As the chapel was not yet finished when the monarchs died, their bodies were buried in what is today the San Francisco Parador hotel, in the Alhambra, where the slab with the inscription of the burial and later transfer of the bodies, in 1521, is still kept.

Charles V was therefore responsible for the completion of the project, which included Renaissance style embellishment and coverings. However, as this building was simple and austere, this king did not actually like it as a place to bury his grandparents. He even stated that it looked more like the tomb of some merchants. Nevertheless, he followed his grandparents' wishes and continued with the project. He even had the remains of his wife (the Empress Isabella) and of his father (King Philip I "The Handsome") brought here, as well as other members of the Royal Family.

When Philip II was on the throne, he was pressurised to have the Royal Chapel annexed to the Cathedral and to move the remains of the monarchs to the latter. The king decided to leave things as they were. He continued the protection of the Chapel, but in his reign it began to lose importance. From then on, the Monastery of

El Escorial would be the place where the Spanish Monarchs were buried. Philip II transferred the remains of his mother, wife, brothers and sisters, who were resting in the Chapel, to El Escorial, although he did not move the remains of his grandmother, Queen Joan "The Mad".

But why did the Catholic Monarchs choose to have their tomb in Granada and not in the cities where they had been born or in the cathedrals of Toledo, Burgos or Leon? It is an indisputable fact that when the monarchs took Granada from the Muslims, on 2 January 1492, they completed the Reconquest process. That is why they wanted to make Granada bigger and better, to demonstrate the victory of Christianity over Islam,

Top right:
Outside view of the Royal Chapel, in the street Calle Oficios, with the Lonja de Mercaderes in the background.

Bottom right:
Part of the exterior facade and doorway of the Royal Chapel.

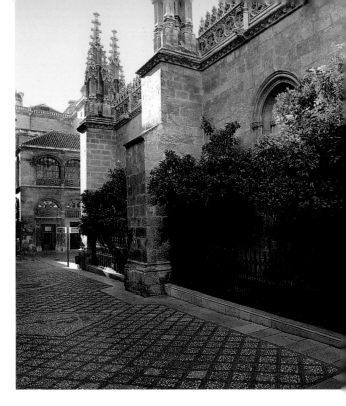

undertaking large constructions that would embellish the city and consolidate its importance in the new age. These are surely enough reasons for building a royal vault here.

THE EXTERIOR FACADE

The top and bottom part of the doorway are clearly differentiated. The top Renaissance style part is previous. It was made in 1527 by the stonemason Juan García de Pradas. It has three niches: the one in the middle has the Madonna and Child and the two on either side contain the two Johns (the Baptist and the Evangelist). The imperial coat of arms is below with the two-headed eagle. The bottom part of the doorway is not original. It was redone by Juan de Aranda in the 18th century. The most striking aspect of the outside walls is the top, where there is "cresting" in the Gothic *"flamigero"* style, which looks like flames. The name *"flamigero"* comes from the Latin "flammiger", which means cast or emit flames. There are ogival windows under the first set of cresting and a frieze under the second. This frieze runs along the entire facade like a border, with the initials F-Y, which stand for Fernando (Ferdinand) and Ysabel (Isabella). The monarchs' coat of arms is above the only window in the facade, with the symbols they adopted in their reign: the yoke and the arrows. "The yoke" represents the equality of the king and the queen, like two oxen pulling the cart together. "The arrows", intertwined, symbolise the union of the two different kingdoms of Spain.

To the left of the chapel's facade, and forming a right angle with it, is the **Lonja de Mercaderes** (a marketplace), whose construction was begun in 1518, in the Gothic style. It is next to, but independent of, the church. It was built for the city's traders to use. The facade of this building, in the Plateresque style, is also the work of Pradas. The ticket office and the entrance to the monument is in the Lonja.

The Catholic Monarchs, the architects of the unity of the kingdoms of Spain

Top:
Praying statues of Isabella I of Castile
and Ferdinand II of Aragon. They are
by Felipe de Bigarny.

Before Isabella and Ferdinand came to the throne, the territory that makes up Spain today was divided into four independent kingdoms: *Castile, Aragon, Navarre and Granada*. The kingdoms of the Crown of Castile and the Crown of Aragon together occupied almost eighty percent of the territory. The Kingdom of Navarre was the smallest and least populated of them all, and the *Kingdom of Granada*, the last territory held by the Muslims left on the peninsula, was the most desirable.

Isabella I of Castile and Ferdinand II of Aragon not only achieved the unity of Spain under the rule of a single reigning monarchy, but they also managed to extend their dominions outside Spanish borders, sometimes thanks to their diplomatic and marriage policy (they married their children off to the heirs to the throne of the main Royal Houses in Europe) and other times due to their military victories. In addition, in their reign and under their flag, America was discovered, and all the territories where Columbus disembarked were added to their crown.

There are two events that marked the lives and the politics of Isabella and Ferdinand, which were decisive in achieving the unity of the kingdoms of Spain and its birth as a modern State: *their marriage and the Conquest of the Kingdom of Granada.*

THE MARRIAGE OF ISABELLA AND FERDINAND AND THE UNION OF THEIR RESPECTIVE CROWNS (CASTILE AND ARAGON)

Until 1469, when their marriage took place, Isabella and Ferdinand had to overcome one difficulty after another, so typical in romantic, and, in this case, almost novel-like, stories. For a start, they were second cousins, so they needed to obtain a papal bull in order to get married. On the other hand, Isabella had several other suitors who were far more important than Ferdinand in the eyes of the Castilian nobles: King Alphonse of Portugal, the Duke of Guienne, the brother of the King of France, and the Duke of Gloucester, the brother of the King of England, apart from some others among the Spaniards. And lastly Ferdinand, who was not popular with the Castilian noblemen, as he was vetoed by Isabella's brother, Henry IV "The Impotent", the King of Castile at the time, and by the all-powerful Marquis of Villena.

What could they do in the face of so many problems? Ferdinand relied on the help of his father, John II of Aragon, and his maternal grandfather, Fadrique Enriquez, the admiral of Castile. But he also managed to get the fearsome archbishop of Toledo, Alonso Carrillo, on his side, who would also be the one to marry them in the end. John II of Aragon gave his son the title of King of Sicily, so that he would be viewed as more valuable by Isabella and the nobles of Castile, a title he used when he got married.

Such was the opposition against Ferdinand that the evil Marquis of Villena even tried to kidnap Isabella and marry her off to Alphonse V of Portugal, and at the same time he tried to use military force to prevent Ferdinand from entering

Castile, where he was going to meet Isabella, who he was apparently already writing to. In view of the size of the opposition, Ferdinand had to keep his wits about him and he entered Castile disguised as a "mule hand" with only four friends as his retinue. Thus the young couple were able to meet at last. Having fallen in love with each other, they became betrothed.

Then there was only the problem of their kinship to resolve, which meant that a "bull" was necessary and, since there was not one at the time, Ferdinand himself and his father John II conspired with the Archbishop Alonso Carrillo to write a false one. It was under the dispensation of this false bull that the marriage was finally celebrated on the nineteenth of December 1469. The real bull was given by Pope Sixtus IV in 1471 two years after the wedding. This marriage finally brought about the union of the Crown of Castile and the Crown of Aragon, which, as a result of the extension of their kingdoms, covered the majority of what is today Spain. Nevertheless, they still did not have the small Kingdom of Navarre and the most desirable of them all, the Nasrid Kingdom of Granada.

THE CONQUEST OF THE NASRID KINGDOM OF GRANADA (1481-1492)

Isabella and Ferdinand, in spite of the hectic political and military life they had to lead, which kept them busy all the time, never forgot Granada, so, as soon as they had solved other hostile fronts in their international politics, they focused their attention on Granada. The fact that the king of Granada, Muley Hacen, had refused to pay the 150,000 maravedis that were stipulated as a tax and that he had started the hostilities by taking the city of Zahara (in Cadiz) by surprise in 1481, sufficed as an excuse to start the war. The astute Spanish monarchs were also able to take advantage of the struggles for power and intrigues raging in the Granadine court between king Muley Hacen, his son (Boabdil) and his brother (the Zagal).

The Catholic Monarchs started a first offensive in response to Muley Hacen's affront when he took the important city of Alhama in 1482, on the frontier of the Granadine kingdom. They took Boabdil prisoner in the battle of Lucena and although they freed him later, it was in exchange

for him proclaiming himself to be a vassal and ally of Castile. Gradually, the most important cities in the kingdom fell into the hands of Ferdinand and Isabella: Ronda in 1485, Loja in 1486, Vélez Málaga and Malaga in 1487. Between 1488 and 1489, they took Huéscar, Vélez Blanco, Vélez Rubio, Baza, Guadix and Almería.

After these conquests, Granada was virtually isolated and in 1491 the Catholic Monarchs asked Boabdil, who was then on the throne, to hand over the city. When the Moorish king refused, the Christians started the siege. They established their camp on Granada's Vega (fertile plain), but a fire started deliberately in the queen's tent razed it to the ground. The Monarchs built a second camp, this time of stone, which they called "Santa Fe" (Holy Faith). Today it is a town on the outskirts of the capital, where the remains of that original royal camp can still be seen. This is where the first meeting between Christopher Columbus and the Monarchs took place and where they signed the "Capitulations". Pursuant to them, the monarchs financed the voyage to the New World for the sailor, but in exchange, they increased the limits of Castile "beyond the seas".

In view of the siege and the strangulation Boabdil was subjected to, he finally ended up accepting the surrender of the city on 2 January 1492. The surrender conditions agreed with Boabdil allowed the Nasrid king to reign in a small territory in the Alpujarras, if he wished. His subjects were granted the right to be judged in accordance with their laws and to keep their way of life, language, property and customs. Some years later, the Monarchs adopted a posture that was not quite so moderate: you either convert to Catholicism or you will be driven out! Right from the start it was Boabdil's intention to leave for Africa. He went out to meet the Catholic Monarchs and their entourage, who were waiting by the banks of the river Genil, and handed over the keys of the city to them.

Isabella I of Castile and Ferdinand II of Aragon had managed to extend their sovereign power to almost all the kingdoms in Spain, as only Navarre was left, which was annexed in 1512. When they conquered the Nasrid kingdom, the dream they had most wished for came true and perhaps that is why their bodies are now resting for ever in this place: "The Royal Chapel of Granada".

CENTRAL NAVE, CHAPELS, MAIN RAILING AND CROSSING

Top:
Top of the Main Railing,
with scenes representing the life of Jesus Christ.

The inside of the Chapel is Gothic style with a ribbed vault, gilded rose windows and capitals made in filigree. The ground-floor plan is only one nave and in the shape of a Latin cross. An enormous railing separates the nave from the crossing. The back door connects with the Church of Sagrario (Tabernacle) and it is Plateresque style, a name which comes from the type of adornments and method of shaping silver used in the 16th century by silversmiths in Spain, which is applied here as architectural ornamentation to the stone sculpting.

At the top and going around the entire Chapel is a sky-blue border with Gothic letters in gold, which tells the story of the foundation and completion of the chapel, as well as historic events, the Catholic Monarchs' conquests and the dates of both their deaths. Under this border is the Monarchs' coat of arms, the yoke and arrows.

There are two chapels closed by exquisite railings on either side of the nave, decorated with the imperial coat of arms. The one on the *left*, at the beginning and under the choir, is the **Capilla de San Ildefonso** (Chapel of St. Ildephonsus). Its railing could be attributed to Bartolomé de Jaén. Worth noting inside are: a Plateresque retable dating from the 16th century, two reliefs representing "the Creation of Eve" and the "Exaltation of the Holy Cross", by Baltasar de Arce, and an "Ecce Homo" bust, by Bernardo de Mora. On the left there is a display cabinet with chalices and other objects of worship. The chapel on the *right*, next to the crossing, is the **Capilla de la**

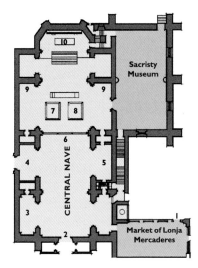

1. Entrance, 2. Sagrario Door, 3. Chapel of St. Ildephonsus,
4. Cathedral Door, 5. Chapel of the Holy Cross,
6. Main Railing, 7. Tomb of King Philip and Queen Joan,
8. Tomb of the Catholic Monarchs, 9. Altar-Reliquaries,
Chancel and High Altar Retable.

Santa Cruz (Chapel of the Holy Cross). We do not know who is responsible for the railing. The retable is Baroque, made by Blas Moreno in 1752. The two busts above the altar, a "Dolorosa" and an "Ecce Homo", are by José Risueño. The Immaculate Conception in the centre is a copy of one by Alonso Cano. Opposite this chapel, on the other side of the nave, is the **Cathedral Door**, with two beautiful sculptures on either side: a "St. John Capistran", by José de Mora, and a "Holy Family

with Saints Anne and Joachim" (Mary, her parents, St. Joseph and Child), by Bernabé de Gaviria.

The Chapel's **main railing,** by Bartolomé de Jaén is in the centre, separating the nave from the crossing. It is made of wrought iron, with embossed fire-gilded and painted plates. It is exactly the same on both sides, except for the "Golgotha Triptych" motif, which has a front and a back. As if it were a retable, it is structured into three storeys or tiers, crowned at the top with small sculptured figures and plant motifs. The main motif of the railing, which is in the centre, is the Catholic Monarchs' coat of arms with the yoke and the arrows and the Gordian knot on either side. There is a complete apostolate on the columns of the second and third tiers with Corinthian capitals.

In the centre of the top section there are scenes representing the Passion of Jesus Christ. The baptism of Jesus by St. John the Baptist and the beheading of this saint are on the left. The martyrdom of St. John the Evangelist is on the extreme right. Above these figures are plant motifs and at the very top there is a triptych of Jesus' crucifixion. A curious fact is that there is an inscription in Latin "maestre Bartolome me fecit" (Master Bartholomew made me) on the left above the first chapter.

Beyond the railing, in the crossing, are the tombs of the Catholic Monarchs and King Philip and Queen Joan, as well as the door of the sacristy-museum and the high altar retable. This will all be referred to below, but first two Baroque altars on either side of the crossing are worth drawing your attention to.

They are **altar-reliquaries**, as the relics of saints, donated to the Catholic Monarchs by popes, are kept behind their doors. They are the work of Alonso de Mena (1630). The one on the *left* has reliefs of the Immaculate Conception, St. John the Baptist, St. Peter and St. Paul engraved on its doors. The bottom section has the Catholic Monarchs, King Philip "The Handsome" and Queen Joan "The Mad". The reliefs on the one on the *right* represent St. Michael, St. James, St. Philip and St. Joseph with Child. At the bottom is Emperor Charles V and his wife Isabella of Portugal, and Philip IV and his wife

Previous page: General view of the nave and the Main Railing of the Royal Chapel.

Top left: Coat of arms of the Catholic Monarchs, the central motif of the railing.

Top right:
"Dolorosa", by Risueño in the Chapel of the Holy Cross.

Bottom: Detail of the doors of the Altar-Reliquary on the left.

Elizabeth Bourbon of France. At the very top of these retables on both sides are figures representing the theological virtues.

THE ROYAL TOMBS

Before describing these royal tombs, we should first tell you something about the people resting underneath in the crypt. As these pages already include a monograph on the Catholic Monarchs, please refer to it for more information. Some notes on the biography of the parents of Emperor Charles V, King Philip and Queen Joan, are below:

Philip I "The Handsome" (1478-1506). The Archduke of Austria and son of Emperor Maximilian I of Austria and Mary of Burgundy. He was the king consort of Spain as a result of his marriage to Joan "The Mad", the daughter of the Catholic Monarchs.

Joan "The Mad" (1479-1555) was the second daughter of the Catholic Monarchs, the Queen of Castile and Aragon. She is known as the Mad because, according to tradition, she lost her mind when her husband, who she was very much in love with, died. Her love for him was so strong that she walked with the funeral cortege throughout all of Castile hoping that Philip would wake up. In 1509 she was confined in Tordesillas (Valladolid) where she stayed until she died.

The tomb of the Catholic Monarchs: this is the lower of the two, the one on the right as you enter. It was made by the Florentine Domenico Alexandro Fancelli, who had made the tomb of Diego Hurtado de Mendoza, the archbishop of Seville.

The Count of Tendilla met with Fancelli and commissioned him with the royal tomb. He made it in Genoa and it was completed in 1517. It is made from Carrara marble. It is

Bottom:
General view of the tombs with the Railing in the background.

quadrangular in plan and the precedent of its shape is the tomb of Pope Sixtus IV, by Pollaiolo. King Ferdinand is on the right and Queen Isabella, whose head is resting lower on the pillow, is on the left. This has led to popular legend saying that the queen was more intelligent than the king, which is why her head weighed more. However, we should honour the truth and remember that the king was perhaps the most intelligent and skilful governor of his time, a true politician, who served as a model for Machiavelli's book "The Prince".

The tomb is decorated with the figures of the first Fathers or Doctors of the Church on the top corners (St. Ambrose, St. Augustine, St. Gregory and St. Jerome). In the middle of the head and sides is the coat of arms of the monarchs and at their feet there is a lion and a lioness (the symbols of royalty and equality) and a cartouche with an inscription in Latin which says: "here lie the monarchs who drove out the Mohammedans, the infidels, etc.". There are medallions with scenes of the life of Jesus, St. George, St. James and sculptures in relief of the twelve apostles on the lower section. The lower corners have figures with the head of an eagle and the body of a lion (griffins).

The tomb of Queen Joan and King Philip: it is the higher of the two, on the left as you enter. It was made by Bartolomé Ordóñez, who was from Burgos, but worked in Naples. The style is more elaborate than that of the other tomb. It was commissioned in 1519. On the top corners are the figures of St. John the Evangelist and St. Michael, St. John the Baptist and St. Andrew. The coats of arms of Spain and Austria are on the sides and at the head. They also have the lion and the lioness at their feet. There are medallions with scenes of the life of Jesus and representations of the virtues on the lower section. The lower corners have symbolic figures, half human at the top and animal at the bottom.

From left to right:
1. St. Andrew. The tomb of Isabella and Ferdinand is in the background.
2. St. Gregory.
3. St. John the Evangelist.
4. Tomb of King Philip and Queen Joan.

161

If you go round this tomb, you can go down some stairs to the crypt, where the bodies lie in lead coffins. The Catholic Monarchs are in the centre, with King Philip and Queen Joan on one side and Prince Michael of Portugal (who was the son of King Manuel of Portugal and

Isabella, the Princess of Asturias, the Catholic Monarchs' eldest daughter, and who died in Granada at the age of two) on the other.

THE HIGH ALTAR RETABLE

As it is on a raised level, it is reached by a staircase with Macael marble banisters, which makes it stand out and appear even higher than it actually is. It is the work of master Felipe de Bigarny, a French artist originally from Burgundy, who was one of the precursors of the Renaissance in Spain. He made it of polychrome wood, in the Plateresque style, between 1520 and 1522.

This breaks with the classic miniaturism of the Spanish retable, which prevailed until the 16th century. The figures are a normal size, influenced by the rise of the figure of man in the Renaissance. There is also no doubt about the influence of the work of Michelangelo in this sculpted group, and of Alonso de Berruguete, who was in Granada at the time and who may well also have worked on it.

Top:
Scene from the Passion of Jesus Christ in the third tier of the Retable.

Bottom:
High Altar Retable in the Royal Chapel.

The bottom section is full of bas-reliefs representing scenes of the conquest of Granada, Boabdil's departure and the baptism of the Moors after the conquest.

In the first tier there are figures representing the Baptism of Jesus, the Adoration of the Magi (centre) and St. John the Evangelist on Patmos.

The second tier is dedicated entirely to the patron saints of this Church, the two Johns (the Evangelist and the Baptist). The figures of them both are in the centre. On the left is the beheading of the Baptist after Salome, who is holding the platter, had asked for his head. On the right is the scene of the martyrdom of the Evangelist, boiled in a cauldron in the reign of Domitian, from which he miraculously emerged alive.

In the third tier there are scenes of the passion and

death of Jesus Christ, with the most outstanding being the large crucifix in the centre, which is the main focal point dominating the entire retable. The figure of God the Father and the dove, the symbol of the Holy Spirit, are in the top crowning piece, which is like a pinnacle (the three figures: the Crucified Son, the Holy Spirit and God the Father represent the mystery of the Blessed Trinity). The Virgin Mary and St. Gabriel, representing the mystery of the Incarnation, are on either side of this third tier above the cornice.

The vertical sections at the ends have large niches with figures of the Apostles and Doctors of the Church. It is all decorated with white and gilded garlands, racemes, little angels and pomegranates, already an indication of the next style to come: Spanish Baroque.

The tabernacle is the work of the great Granadine woodcarver Domingo Sánchez

On the whole page:
Bas-reliefs from the bottom section of the Altar with scenes of the baptism of Moors, the conquest of Granada and the departure of Boabdil.

Left:

General view of the Sacristy. It is divided into two sections: the first is for gold and silverware and cloth items. The second is for Queen Isabella's important painting collection.

Bottom:

Queen Isabella's sceptre and King Ferdinand's ceremonial sword.

Queen Isabella's crown.

Queen Isabella's jewellery box, in gilded silver with Gothic motifs.

Mesa. Below on either side are the praying statues of the Catholic Monarchs, by Diego de Siloé.

THE SACRISTY-MUSEUM

The Gothic style doorway leading to it is by Jacobo Florentino, as is the Annunciation above it. Inside it is divided into two. The first contains gold and silverware and fabric articles. The second contains the Chapel's important collection of paintings, the property of Queen Isabella.

The **gold and silverware** are mainly personal objects belonging to the monarchs, such as Queen Isabella's legendary jewellery box in gilded silver with Gothic motifs and the Queen's missal, with its silver case. The queen's sceptre and crown and King Ferdinand's ceremonial sword are in the centre in a display case. There are also numerous religious items, such as an altar cross, paxes, chalices and a monstrance, made from what was once Queen Isabella's mirror.

The **cloth items** include altar frontals, a chasuble of the vestments known as the "chapao" or of the Catholic King, vestments of black chasubles, which were the ones used to accompany the wife of Charles V on her journey from Toledo to Granada to be buried in the Royal Chapel. The sacristy also contains the standards and banners the Christian troops were carrying when they entered Granada in 1492.

The second section of the room is used for the important **painting collection**. Queen Isabella the Catholic made it clear in her will that when she died, her private collection of paintings was to be transferred to Granada so that it could decorate the chapel she was having built as her burial place. These panels (they are pictures painted on wood) are the sacristy's great treasure and form a unique collection in Europe as a result of their variety and their extraordinary historic, artistic and sentimental value.

The best work here is a retable, the "Triptych of the Passion". The retable is the work of Jacobo Florentino and the paintings in the centre (*Crucifixion, Deposition and Resurrection*) are by Dieric Bouts. The other paintings that form it, above and below, are by Jacobo Florentino and Pedro Machuca. The praying statues of Ferdinand and Isabella, the work of Bigarny, are on either side of the retable.

The majority of the panels belong to the Flemish school, and the most outstanding of them are: two pictures by Rogier Van der Weyden (1400-1464), "The Nativity" and "The Pietà", which form part of a triptych. The third painting in this triptych "Christ Appearing to His Mother" is in the Metropolitan Museum, in New York.

Another great artist of this school here is the German Hans Memling (1430-1494), with the diptych "The Deposition" and "The Lamentation". He also painted "Madonna and Child Enthroned" and "The Pietà".

Top: *"St. John the Baptist".* Painter: Jan Provost.

"Seated Madonna and Child Accompanied by Four Angels". Painter: Dieric Bouts.

Left: *Retable of the "Triptych of the Passion", which dominates the painting collection in this sacristy. The praying statues of the monarchs are the work of Bigarny.*

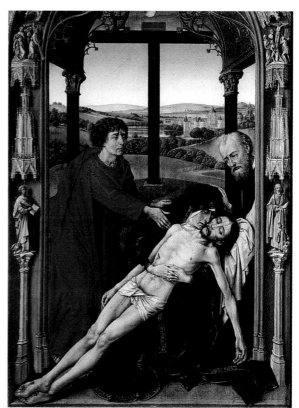

Top:
Bust of Christ. Anonymous painter.

Right (top and bottom):
"The Nativity" and "The Pietà".
Both paintings form part of the "Triptych
of the Virgin" by Rogier Van der Weyden.
The third painting in this triptych,
"Christ Appearing to His Mother",
is in the Metropolitan Museum.

Dieric Bouts (1410-1475), who was Dutch and a disciple of Van der Weyden, is, apart from the great retable "Triptych of the Passion", already mentioned above and which dominates the room, also responsible for the painting "Seated Madonna and Child Accompanied by Four Angels". There is another painting, "Bust of Christ", usually attributed to Dieric Bouts, but considered by other researchers as by some anonymous follower of his.

There are also a great number of panels by anonymous painters, contemporary to the others: "St. John the Baptist", "St. Michael", "The Penitent St. Jerome", "Madonna and Child with Two Angels" and some others. The most noteworthy among them is an "Annunciation", attributed to Antonio Alemán.

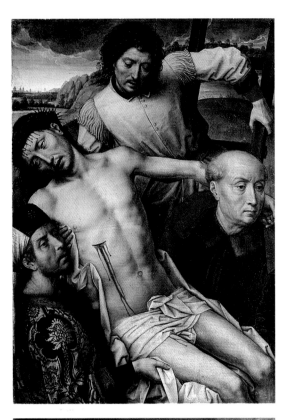

Top:
"Madonna and Child Enthroned"
by Hans Memling.

Left (top and bottom):
"The Deposition" and "The Lamentation".
Both form part of a diptych and are the
work of Hans Memling.

Worth noting from the Italian school are Pietro Perugino (1445-1523), the master of Raphael, with his "Ecce Homo", and Sandro Botticelli (1444-1510) with his "The Agony in the Garden".

The Spanish School is represented by Pedro Berruguete with "St. John the Evangelist on Patmos" and Bartolomé Bermejo with two paintings on the front and back of a panel "Epiphany" and "Holy Face". Queen Isabella was very fond of this painting, as she took it with her whenever she travelled.

Some of the paintings, together with the Archive, where around one hundred and forty manuscripts from the Queen's library, papal bulls and royal warrants are kept, were plundered by Philip II to enhance the Monastery of El Escorial and the Simancas Archive.

"The Pietà". Painter. Hans Memling.

OTHER MONUMENTS
of interest

The three monuments described on these pages are very close to each other and further increase the vast historical and monumental interest in this area.

The Church of Sagrario

It is located on the former site of the main Mosque of Granada. The former Mosque was built at the beginning of the 11th century and it looked like a simple and poor building at first. Later it was altered and its decoration and materials were upgraded, so that it became one of the richest and most emblematic buildings in Muslim Granada. It measured 140 by 110 metres, with an orange tree courtyard and a thirteen metre high minaret. In Christian times (1501) a parish church was established dedicated to Santa María de la O (Our Lady of O). In 1704 what was left of the Mosque was knocked down, as in previous years, many parts of it had been demolished or modified. Work on the current church was started in 1705, under the management of Francisco Hurtado Izquierdo, but then halted due to a lack of funds. It was resumed in 1717, under the management of José de Bada. The new church was opened for worship on 29 September 1759.

The main doorway, made of marble from Sierra Elvira, is formed by two sections, with Corinthian columns on either side. The top section, above the door arch, has sculptures of St. Peter, St. Ives and St. John Nepomucene, the work of Agustín Vera Moreno.

The plan is a Greek cross within a square. A large central cupola covers the section in the middle, with the roofs of the four side sections surrounding it. It is perhaps this play of geometry and shapes you notice most when you look up at the ceiling of this singular church. There are recesses in the four large columns

supporting the cupola with Baroque adornments and sculptures of the four evangelists inside, made by Vera Moreno. There is a predominant colour throughout the church: the colour of stone, which was very much in vogue in the Neoclassical period.

The centre of the high altar is taken up by a marble tabernacle (which is what the name of this church, *Sagrario,* means) by José de Bada. The small figures adorning it represent the Fathers of the Church and crowning it is the figure of Faith. Behind the tabernacle, in the centre of the apse, there is a Baroque retable with the image of St. Peter. The marble sculptures of the archangels St. Michael and St. Raphael are on either side above the doors connecting with the sacristy.

There is a large painting of "St. Joseph with Child" in the top part of the apse and the marble figures of St. Joachim and St. Anne are at the sides. All these marble sculptures are by Tomás Valero.

The most significant of the side chapels is probably the one dedicated to Hernán Pérez del Pulgar, due to its historical symbolism, in remembrance of his feat. On 18 December 1490, when Granada was still ruled by the Muslims, he slipped into the heart of the city and plunged a dagger with a parchment into the main door of the Mosque. The parchment contained the words "Ave Maria" and recorded the fact that from that moment, and in honour of the Blessed Virgin, the Mosque had been taken for Christianity (at least symbolically). Pérez del Pulgar is actually buried in this chapel, located today in the place where this achievement took place so many years ago. The railing, which has the coat of arms of Charles V, is by Bartolomé de Jaén (1526).

Distinguished people are buried in this church, such as the princes Don Pedro and Don Alonso of Granada; Fray Hernando de Talavera,

Previous page:
Facade of the Church
of Sagrario and the inside
of the church.

Top:
Detail of the ceiling of the
church.

the city's first archbishop, Ana de Santotis, Diego de Siloé's first wife, and the architect Ambrosio de Vico.

The Madraza or Old City Hall

There is not much still standing today of this Madraza, or Arab University, built under the orders of Yusuf I in 1349, and it has been heavily restored. Theology, Law, Medicine, Literature and Mathematics were studied here. As was usual in the majority of the Muslim madrazas, it had a large doorway, a central courtyard with a pool in the middle and cells around it for the students and classrooms. The oratory used to be at the back of the central courtyard. According to the chronicles, the Granadine Madraza had an extremely long tradition, as it was the oldest in Muslim Spain. When it was founded it was located elsewhere, on a royal estate outside Granada.

Since as early as the days of the Catholic Monarchs, numerous modifications have been undertaken, which ended up demolishing almost the entire building and constructing another completely new one. What we can see today is a building dating from the beginning of the 18th century, with the remains of rooms from other ages. Most worth noting are the **Salón de Caballeros Veinticuatro** (16th century), with a magnificent Mudéjar ceiling, and the **Oratory**. The *facade* is also worth an express mention due to the ornamental paintings covering it, which, with their play of volumes and shapes, make it one of the most curious of Granadine Baroque. It was the location of the City Hall of Granada from when the new building

Top left:
Cupola of the oratory of the Madraza.

Top right:
Detail of the Mihrab, in the Oratory.

Bottom:
Facade of the Palace of Madraza
or the Old City Hall.

was erected in 1729 to 1851, the date when it was transferred to its current site. That is why this monument is also known as the "Old City Hall".

The only example of Muslim art in the entire monument is the *oratory*, located in the courtyard, which you enter as you go in. Nevertheless, what you can see today is not its original state, since the Christians distorted it almost completely when they converted it into a chapel. It was therefore virtually totally redone in 1893. Despite this fact, its unquestionable beauty and what it represents make it one of the places that best evoke the past Nasrid magic of this city.

The Corral del Carbón

In Muslim times this place that is nowadays called the "coal yard" was known as *Alhóndiga Gidida* or *Nueva* (Gidida or New Corn Exchange) at the start of the 14th century. It is thought that it served two purposes: a storage facility for goods and a "fondak" (guesthouse), where the merchants stayed. The Muslims were extremely hospitable, but when a stranger could not find a bed in the house of a relative or friend, he stayed overnight in the "fondak". After the Christian conquest, the Catholic Monarchs gave it to one of their servants and after his death without heirs, the building was auctioned. Since then to our times, it has had many different uses. The merchants who traded coal used it as somewhere

to stay, as the place where this merchandise was weighed was not very far from here. This is how it got its current name. Later it was used for open-air theatre performances. In the 17th century it was a tenement house until finally, in 1933, the State acquired it and started the restoration, as it had greatly deteriorated.

The best part of the building is the doorway, which is very richly decorated. It has a large pointed horseshoe arch leading to a small hall with a muqarna vault and the front door, which is rectangular. Two coupled windows crown the arch and the door, providing the whole with movement. Inside there is a large courtyard with a fountain in the centre, and around it there is a gallery of several storeys with many small rooms or chambers leading off it.

Top:
Exterior facade of the Corral del Carbón.

Left:
Interior courtyard of the Corral del Carbón.

The Monasteries of Cartuja and San Jerónimo

MONOGRAPHS INCLUDED

MAP OF THE AREA

① MONASTERY OF CARTUJA
PAGE 178

② ROYAL HOSPITAL
PAGE 206

③ BASILICA OF SAN JUAN DE DIOS
PAGE 208

④ PLAZA DE LA UNIVERSIDAD
PAGE 210

⑤ MONASTERY OF SAN JERÓNIMO
PAGE 194

Map labels:
Al Monasterio de La Cartuja
Paseo de la Cartuja
Real de Cartuja
Avenida de Murcia
Acera de S. Ildefonso
Cuesta del Hospicio
Avda. C. Moreno
Ancha de Capuchinos
Plaza del Triunfo
Avda. D. Pastora
Plaza S. Isidro
Avenida de Madrid
Avenida de la Constitución
San Juan de Dios
Gran Vía de Colón
Santa Paula
Alhambra Albaicín
Catedral
San Jerónimo
Plaza Universidad
Santa Bárbara
Dr. Severo Ochoa
Rector López Argüeta
Calle de la Duquesa
Plaza de los Lobos
Gran Capitán
Carril del Picón
Avenida Fuente Nueva
Melchor Almagro
Martínez de la Rosa
Plaza Gran Capitán
E. Eugenia

MAIN MONUMENTS

Shown with a photograph on the map.

OTHER PLACES TO VISIT:

6.- Church of San Ildefonso. .... P. 117
7.- Hospital of San Juan de Dios. .... P. 117
8.- Church of Perpetuo Socorro. .... P. 117
9.- Hall of residence of San Bartolomé y Santiago. .... P. 117
10.- Victoria Eugenia music conservatory. .... P. 117
11.- Colegio Notarial (Notary Association). .... P. 117

USEFUL INFORMATION:

– The Monastery of Cartuja (number 1) and the Monastery of San Jerónimo (number 5) are the two most important monuments in this chapter and are well worth a visit.

INTRODUCTION
and itinerary

Granada has many convents and monasteries.
These pages cover the two most important.

Granada is full of old convents and monasteries. The two dealt with here, the Monasteries of **Cartuja** (Carthusian) and of **San Jerónimo** (St. Jerome) are undoubtedly the two most important, with exceptional churches due to their beauty and historic-artistic value.

This "route of the monasteries" goes around the city centre to the north-west and, except for the surroundings of *Cartuja Monastery*, the majority of the route runs very close to the Cathedral area. The fact that "Cartujas" (Carthusian Monasteries) were always built on the outskirts of cities forces us to leave the centre of Granada. But even so, the distance between the two monuments furthest away from each other on the map in this chapter can be walked in twenty minutes. We recommend starting with *Cartuja Monastery* and finishing with the *Monastery of San Jerónimo*, at the opposite end.

Other suggestions for this itinerary are included in the section **"Other monuments of interest"**. They are: the **Hospital Real,** built by the Catholic Monarchs as a refuge hospital for the sick and destitute. It currently houses the central services of the University of Granada; the **Church of San Juan de Dios** (St. John of God), dating from the 18th century, one of the most sumptuous temples of Granadine Baroque; the square called **Plaza de la Universidad**, where the **Church of San Justo y Pastor** (St. Justus and Pastor) stands, dating from the 16th and 17th centuries, and the current **Facultad de Derecho** (Faculty of Law), the former Literary University, which was the university headquarters from 1769 to 1980.

If you have time, stop off at some other interesting places and monuments in this area, which are very close to each other: The **Church of San Ildefonso** (St. Ildephonsus), which is very near the *Royal Hospital*, a former mosque built on the outskirts of the city to meet the needs of the Albaycin's furthermost district. The **Hospital of San Juan de Dios** next to the church with the same name, built and run by the hieronymite monks in the 16th century and later transferred to the brothers of this hospital order. The

Top:
View of the surroundings of the Plaza de la Universidad, with the cupola of the Church of San Justo y Pastor in the background.

courtyard that follows on from the entrance hall and the staircase, with its Mudéjar ceiling, are extremely beautiful. The **Church of Perpetuo Socorro** (Perpetual Help), dating from the 17th and 18th centuries, originally dedicated to St. Philip Neri. It was later equipped as a church of the Redemptorist Fathers and then dedicated to Our Lady of Perpetual Help. The **Colegio Mayor de San Bartolomé y Santiago** (Hall of Residence of St. Bartholomew and James), a university foundation dating from the 17th century. Opposite is the **Conservatorio de Música Victoria Eugenia** (Music Conservatory) in the former small palace belonging to the Marquises of Caicedo, dating from the 16th century. The **Colegio Notarial** (Notary Association), in the former palace of the Ansotis, dating from the 17th century. The latter are all in Calle San Jerónimo, from where it meets Calle San Juan de Dios to Plaza de la Universidad.

THE MONASTERY OF
Cartuja

*Few places in Granada surprise visitors as
much as the church and sacristy of this monument*

Previous page:
*Gate of the monastery with the
church in the background.*

Top:
Detail of the outside of the church.

Bottom:
Detail of the inside of the Sacristy.

t is curious to note that this monastery was built on the grounds of an Arab recreational estate. This Arab "carmen" was called *Aynadamar* or *Source of Tears*, and the Christian conquerors were amazed by how plentiful the water and fruit trees were. The Great Captain himself, Don Gonzalo Fernández de Córdoba, caught sight of the city of Granada for the first time from the beautiful estate of *Aynadamar*, and he was also attacked here by surprise by a group of Moors, miraculously surviving unhurt. That is why he decided to build "a house devoted to God where He is served and adored at all hours" in this place.

While all this was happening, the Community of the Carthusian Order of El Paular had made a decision to build a new Carthusian Monastery, dependent on this community, but they had not yet found a specific site. This project ended up being shelved, although after a few years it resurfaced, and new land was sought in Galicia, Castile and Leon. Excavations were even started in Zamora, but the monks were not successful in this second attempt to build a new monastery either.

In view of the difficulty in finding a definitive location, Father Juan Padilla, the prior of the monastery Cartuja de las Cuevas in Seville and Visitor of the Order, turned to Don Gonzalo Fernández de Córdoba and his wife for help. The Great Captain not only proposed building the Carthusian Monastery in the grounds of the Aynadamar estate, but he even offered to take charge of the project, with the initial idea of being buried in this new monastery. The donation of this land was made in Loja in 1513. Several difficulties interrupted the work, among them the Great Captain's death in 1515. Nevertheless, before he died, he had had some disagreements with the monks, which made him change his mind about being buried here. Work was resumed again in 1519. In 1545, the Carthusian Monastery of Granada was incorporated into the Order, and has been known since then by the name of *Asunción de Nuestra Señora*

(Assumption of Our Lady), and Father Rodrigo de Valdepeñas was appointed the first prior.

All that is left of the entire monastery today are the *Small Cloister, Church, Tabernacle and Sacristy*, since the rest of it (large cloister, cells, workshops and cemetery) mostly disappeared in 1842, as it suffered during the invasion of the French troops and the Disentailment (The Disentailment was expropriation of the property of religious orders, decreed by the State in 1837, which was handed over to private individuals in most cases). The Priory House, which had a beautiful courtyard and a small garden, was also destroyed in 1943. Nowadays, the monastery does not belong to the Carthusian Order, but depends directly on the Archbishopric and Diocese of Granada.

The entrance to the Monastery is a small Plateresque gate, made by Juan García de Pradas in 1520. From the entrance you can see a double stone staircase and the facade of the church rising above its final landing, which are all the work of the stonemason Cristóbal de Vílchez. Two elements of the facade are worth noting. The

most significant is the door. It stands between columns made of marble from Sierra Elvira and the statue of the founder, St. Bruno, by Pedro Hermoso, is at the top. The other element is the coat of arms of Spain from the Bourbon age. Once inside, the route followed takes you to the Cloister first, then the Church, the Sancta Sanctorum and the Sacristy.

Nevertheless, before going on to the description of these parts of the monastery, perhaps it would be useful to stop and read the monograph on the following pages about St. Bruno, the founder of the Order, and the way of life of the monks who lived within these walls all those years ago.

St. Bruno and the way of life of the Carthusians

The Carthusian Order arouse around the figure of *St. Bruno*, who was born in Cologne in 1027. He studied at the cathedral school of Reims and eventually became the chancellor and master of this cathedral. He did not feel very comfortable with life in the city or with the scandals that went on there, so he decided on a complete change and moved to the region of Grenoble. There, his bishop, the future St. Hugh, provided him with a place in the French Alps, at an altitude of 1,084 metres, so that he could build a "hermitage" (a place of retreat where he could lift up his soul to God) with six companions. The "hermitage" consisted of several wooden cabins, where every one of them lived in absolute solitude, and which opened onto a sort of gallery, where part of their shared life together took place. This site was in Chartreuse valley, which is where the order got its name from.

After six years, Pope Urban II called Bruno to him as an adviser. However, he was only in Rome for a few months, as life at the pontifical court did not interest him in the slightest. He even rejected the archbishopric of Reggio Calabria, offered to him by the Pope, who therefore suggested that he found another hermitage in the woods of Calabria, in the south of Italy. Bruno died in this new hermitage on the sixth of October 1101. The Order of the Carthusians officially came into being in 1140, during the priorate of St. Anthelm.

Top:
The small sculpture of St. Bruno by José de Mora. It is considered one of the best images of Spanish Baroque.

THE WAY OF LIFE OF THE CARTHUSIANS

The main purpose of a Carthusian's life is "contemplation", and to achieve this end solitude is the most important characteristic in their lives. The community was formed by *monks* and *lay brothers*. The monks lived in the strictest solitude, only leaving their cells on specific planned occasions. The lay brothers' task was to serve the community and do the routine jobs, so they spent more time outside their cells. The waiting period before being ordained was long, about nineteen years as a novice, donné or postulant. Later the time was decreased to eleven years and today it is about seven and a half years.

The monks did not leave their cells except for the daily liturgy, for lunch on Sundays and on very few occasions when they had to get together to deliberate or make decisions. The majority of their life was spent in their cells, where they prayed, ate, read and did their chores. When the monks had to deliberate they met in the Chapter House. Here they were told about any deaths and intentions they had been entrusted, but without any names being mentioned. When someone wanted to enter the order, they discussed whether another person was needed or not. Every monk was given a white and a black kidney bean. The voting was always done in secret by putting the kidney bean into a wooden box, white if the vote was in favour and black if it was against.

Not very far from the Chapter House and from the entrance to the church, there was the so-called "Tabula", which existed in all the Carthusian monasteries. The tabula was a large tablet on which all the directives regarding the teachings of the trades and of life in the community were written. Monks could read the specific instructions on this tablet without having to ask anyone anything, which was forbidden by the rule of the "vote of silence".

The lay brothers' task was to ensure that their work covered the community's different requirements, such as cooking, carpentry, gardening, etc. In general, each one had a manual job and they were great craftsmen. They met in their own Chapter House. They had to take the monks their meals in their cells, except on Sundays or special community holidays, when they ate in the dinning hall or refectory. They were not allowed to speak to a brother, or enter his cell, as this was forbidden, and the

monks cleaned their cells themselves and left their dirty washing at the door, once a week, so that the lay brothers could collect it. Lay brothers were allowed to grow beards, but they were only allowed to shave on the days the Carthusian calendar indicated. However, their diet was exactly the same as the monks'.

Carthusians ate just one full meal a day, as they only had a bit of bread and water at night. On Fridays they only ate bread and water, and during their Lent, which lasted from the middle of September until Easter, they had nothing for dinner at all. Eating meat was forbidden for life, even if it had been prescribed medically. Every monk was allowed to drink half a litre of wine per day, except on Fridays, when they only had a jug of water and a bit of bread for their meals. This was changed to another day if Friday was a holiday. They also refrained from eating dairy products during Advent and Lent.

When the meal was eaten in the refectory (Sundays and special occasions), there was a reader who read out prayers during the meal and who only ate when it had finished. He was also responsible for distributing half a loaf to each monk as he went into the refectory. Nobody could ask for anything for himself, but if one of them needed something, he could indicate this with a signal. The Father General ate at a table alone, presided over by the Great Crucifix. Monks and lay brothers ate in the same room, but separated by a wooden grille.

There is a curious anecdote about the Carthusians' strict diet and the fact that eating meat was forbidden. Blessed Pope Urban V (1309-1370) wanted to change this rule of not eating meat for life, as he thought it could be damaging to the Carthusians' health. The monks, who feared these good papal intentions, as they thought they would weaken their discipline, sent representatives, on foot, to protest to Urban V. The above-mentioned representatives were twenty-seven monks, aged between 88 and 95. The Pope immediately abandoned the idea (no comment!). Ref. Robin Bruce Lockhart "Halfway to Heaven", page 119.

Left:
The monastery's cloister.

Right:
Detail of the fountain in the centre of the cloister.

THE CLOISTER AND ITS ROOMS

This small cloister is the only one still standing, as there were two originally. The larger one, around which the cells were located and which had the community's cemetery in the centre, disappeared. The monks were buried there according to Carthusian ritual, in other words, without a coffin, on a board and wearing a smock. That is why this cloister is known in Spanish as the "claustrillo", which means small cloister.

It is square in plan with Doric style columns, made of grey stone from Sierra Elvira. It served as a meeting point for the monks, as the *Refectory, monks' Chapter House, De Profundis Chapel* and the *lay brothers' Chapter House* are here. It was also used as a way to go to the religious services in the church. It is the oldest part, prior to the construction of the church, and all its rooms, which are

Gothic in style, have been preserved. It has contagious charm and its orange trees, rose bushes and aromatic plants with the fountain in the centre remind us more of an Arab or Andalusian courtyard than a cloistered monastery.

A Carthusian's daily life was divided into two blocks: the solitary life (most of the time), which was spent in the privacy of his cell, and community life, which occurred between the church and this cloister, including the rooms around it. (Bear the notes on the way of life of the Carthusians in mind when you go around these rooms).

The first room you come across is the **"refectory"** or **dining hall**. The head of John the Baptist after his beheading is on a platter above the door, as if it were an invitation to forget the pleasures of food. The paintings in this

room are by Sánchez Cotán. The first one worth mentioning is the one dominating the room: "The Last Supper", where the marvellous realism of the windows is striking. Also curious in this painting is the fact that Cotán painted a fish on Jesus' plate instead of lamb, as Carthusians are never allowed to eat meat, and the dog and the cat are eating its backbone. The cross above the painting, which seems to be made of wood, is actually painted on the wall. Other paintings to notice are: the one representing "St. Bruno Becoming a Carthusian"; a painting depicting the terror of Raimundo de Diocres waking up in the middle of his funeral saying that he was condemned to the eternal fire, when everyone thought he was a saintly man; and "The Dream of Hugh, Bishop of Grenoble", in which seven stars, representing St. Bruno and his six companions (the first founders) appear to him in dreams. These companions were: Landuin, Stephen of Die, Stephen of Bourg and Hugh (brothers); Andrew and Guerin (laymen). Please refer to the biography on St. Bruno for more information. The rest of the paintings represent the persecutions and executions of the monks in England by Henry VIII and the Huguenots in France. Take a look at the one representing horses dragging the monks. Due to an optical effect, the horses seem to change direction in this painting, depending on where you look at it from.

The **"De Profundis" Chapel** is the next room. This is where the monks did penance and asked God for forgiveness. The name "De Profundis" comes from Psalm 130, in which David begs for mercy and submits to penance. It is a simple room where there is an altar painted in relief on the wall and a painting of St. Peter and St. Paul, all by Fray Juan Sánchez Cotán, who signed "Joannes Fecit" on St. Paul's sword. The fact that the altar is painted in relief is important, as the effect is real, and the use of expensive construction materials is not necessary. No fine materials were ever used in the part for the Carthusians, as these were reserved for the Glory of God.

Fray Sánchez Cotán was born in Orgaz (Toledo) in 1560. He was influenced by Navarrete and El Greco and became a great specialist in still lifes, as well as in religious subjects. He was the great predecessor of Zubarán. In 1603 he went to the Monastery of El Paular, becoming a lay brother. In 1610-1612 he came to Granada, where he was known as "Santo Fray Juan". He left a large collection of paintings kept in the Monastery and in the Fine Arts Museum in Granada. He died in this city in 1627.

Next, you enter the **lay brothers' Chapter House** through a small Gothic door. This is where the lay brothers met, who were responsible, as mentioned before, for serving the community. The paintings in here are by Vicente Carducho. Next to it is the **monks' Chapter House**. This is where the monks met to deliberate and where sermons were given. The paintings in the room are also by Carducho, dating from the 17th century. Note the acoustics of this room.

Left:
"De Profundis" Chapel, with the painting of St. Peter and St. Paul and the altar painted in relief, both by Sánchez Cotán.

Right:
Blessed Ford's Vision, in the monks' chapter house, by Vicente Carducho.

THE CHURCH

The Baroque style design, dating from around 1662, is divided into three well defined sections: *the first*, from the main door to the gate, was for the faithful. The emblem of the order (the seven allegorical stars representing St. Bruno and his six companions, when they withdrew to live in the place called Chartreuse, near Grenoble, in 1084) is above the door.

The second, from the gate to the marquetry door, was for the lay brothers. The marquetry door was made in 1750 by the best marquetry craftsman there has ever been: the lay brother Fray José Manuel Vázquez. There are two Baroque retables on either side of the door, with paintings by Sánchez Cotán, from around 1612, which represent: "The Holy Family Resting on the Flight to Egypt" and "The Baptism of Jesus". Notice the surprising realism in the detail of the bread, cheese and knife in the first of these two paintings. The two altars are made of a single piece of marble from Lanjarón. There are also plaster statues of Biblical figures in the top section.

The third section the church is divided into is reserved for the monks, and it is just behind this door. It is totally cut off from the rest of the church, as prescribed by the Carthusian monks' complete religious seclusion for life. Even the seats where the monks sat are high, so that they could not see each other. Note that there is no choir. Neither is there an organ, as musical instruments were strictly forbidden by the Order. The only music that there may have been within these walls in the past was the chanting of the monks in

Top:
Baroque retable with paintings by Sánchez Cotán and the marquetry door. It led to the part of the church reserved for the monks.

Next page:
General view of the church.

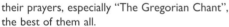

their prayers, especially "The Gregorian Chant", the best of them all.

The monks entered the church through another door further along, on the right. The church was only used by the monks as a community, five times a day. The first time was at midnight, until half past two, when they returned to their cells. Then again at seven and eleven o'clock in the morning. After lunch, and a short rest, they went back to the church at around half past three in the afternoon and then again to do "all the Hours of the Great Office" and "the Office of Our Lady", which ended about seven o'clock, the time when they usually went back to their cells to go to bed.

The extreme whiteness of the walls is a characteristic of Carthusian churches. Among the works of art here are the collection of paintings of the Virgin Mary, painted by Pedro Atanasio Bocanegra (a disciple of Alonso Cano) in the 17th century. His most beautiful work is a little bit further on the left, framed by marble from Lanjarón: "Our Lady of the Rosary". The cupola, with figures of the Evangelists and lanterns which light passes through to shine on the altar, is undoubtedly Baroque. The top part of the entire church depicts biblical figures.

The section behind the altar in the church is polychrome with statues of St. John the Baptist, the Patron of the Order, on the left and St. Bruno, the founder, on the right. In the middle there is an Assumption by José de Mora, framed by a gilded wooden baldachin inlaid with glass. The baldachin is the work of Francisco Hurtado, dated 1710.

THE SANCTA SANCTORUM

This is located behind the altar and it is where relics and the sacred species are kept. It is by Hurtado Izquierdo and Baroque in style, although verging on Rococo. It was finished around 1720 and the two side chapels date from around 1725. Its most surprising feature is the exuberant decoration, with an abundant use of marble from Lanjarón and Cabra. The door is made of Venetian glass.

There is a marble **baldachin** in the centre with black Solomonic style columns and an inlaid palm tree inside. There are four statues at the corners, which, according to Emilio Orozco, are the work of Duque Cornejo, and which represent the four virtues: justice, prudence, fortitude and temperance. At the very top of it all is the figure of the theological virtue of faith, by Risueño. The tabernacle case inside, made of precious wood, was made in 1816. The original, which was made of silver and glass, was stolen by General Sebastiani during the French occupation.

There are four statues in the corners of the interior: St. Bruno, St. John the Baptist, Mary Magdalene and St. Joseph with Child, which are by José de Mora (St. Bruno and St. Joseph), Risueño (St. John the Baptist) and by Duque Cornejo (Mary Magdalene). These statues are under some canopies, which, as they are polychrome and tasselled, give us the impression that they are made of velvet or silk. However, they are made of wood, thus emphasising the "optical effect" of unreality. These canopies are the work of Duque Cornejo.

There are some oeils-de-boeuf, which link with two chapels, on either side in the lower section, through which the monks could worship the Blessed Sacrament.

One of its most beautiful elements is without a doubt the **cupola**, with fresco paintings by Antonio Palomino and José Risueño, in which the Blessed Sacrament of the Eucharist is extolled, with St. Bruno holding a globe on which there is a monstrance. The four Evangelists are represented in the four corners supporting the cupola or "squinches", each one with their symbol: St. John with the eagle, St. Mark with the lion, St. Luke with the ox and St. Matthew with the angel.

Worth noticing is the extraordinary flooring, also made of marble and stone, and the paintings by Palomino, representing "David and Abigail" and "Moses Circumcising his Sons".

Right:
Detail of the different Virtues decorating the Sancta Sanctorum.

SACRISTY

On leaving the Sancta Sanctorum, on the right, and behind a smooth door with marquetry inlay, you come to the "Sacristy". There are times when art does not need to be explained, as great beauty and harmony speak for themselves. Having visited the cloister, the church and the Sancta Sanctorum, you may have thought that there was nothing else to see, but the best was yet to come. It is as if, on going over the threshold, you have walked into the finale of "Beethoven's Ninth Symphony" or into the adagio of "Bruckner's Seventh Symphony". On entering the Sacristy you realise that the final word had not been said. The bright whiteness envelops you, taking you to a purer, more ethereal dimension, where any comments would be pointless.

So, we will simply mention who the creators of this brilliant work were. The carver Luis Ca-

Previous page:
Impressive cupola covering
the Sancta Sanctorum with fresco paintings.

Top:
Detail of the sacristy's ceiling.

bello was responsible for the stucco and the stonemason Luis de Arévalo worked the rich marble from Lanjarón forming the surround, with strange figures tracing the veins in the marble: a cat's head, a dog's head, a fish, a young woman seated with flowers in her hair, which makes us wonder if they are real or painted. The cupola, in no way inferior to the rest, is by Tomás Ferrer. There are two sculptures in the centre of the retable: an alabaster Immaculate Conception and

Top:
Detail of one of the vestment cases decorating the sacristy. They are by the lay brother Fray José Manuel Vázquez.

Bottom:
Detail of the sacristy's door.

Next page:
General view of the sacristy.

a St. Bruno. However, these sculptures, of average artistic merit, are not the best artwork to be found here, as the most exceptional and valuable piece is the small image of St. Bruno at the back on the left, by the Granadine sculptor José de Mora. Originally, it was not designed for the sacristy nor located here. It is considered one of the best Baroque images due to its poignant spirituality.

The decorative elements that probably catch visitors' attention the most in this sacristy are the marvellous marquetry vestment cases. They were crafted by the lay brother Fray José Manuel Vázquez, and they are made of mahogany, ebony, guaiacum, ivory, mother-of-pearl, tortoiseshell and silver. It took him no less than thirty-four years to complete them, from 1730 to 1764. And after almost three centuries, the wood and inlay work still look as if they were made yesterday and will last for many years to come.

Lastly, we would just like to point out that this sacristy of the Carthusian Monastery in Granada seems to be a direct descendant of the Alhambra judging by its stucco, marquetry and imagination.

THE MONASTERY OF
San Jerónimo

As you enter this monument in the middle of the bustling city you go back 500 years in time to the 16th century, when it was built and also when the "Great Captain", whose mortal remains are resting here, was alive.

The first Order of St. Jerome in Granada was located in Real de Santa Fe in the Convento de Santa Catalina (Monastery of St. Catherine), when the Catholic Monarchs set up their camp there to lay siege while waiting for surrender. But after the site was abandoned, the monks were left to fend for themselves until the Monarchs offered the three most important religious orders of the day (Franciscans, Dominicans and Hieronymites) a place in the city after it had been colonised so that they could establish their monasteries there. The Hieronymites were granted a place called "El Nublo", which is now the Hospital of San Juan de Dios (St. John of God).

The chronicles say that the Hieronymites arrived so lacerated and bitten by insects that "they did not look like the monks of St. Jerome at all, but rather of St. Lazarus" (the monks of St. Lazarus were the ones who looked after people with leprosy). It is not known whether these misfortunes befell the Hieronymites in the place called "El Nublo" or in what was left of Santa Fe. However, in 1496, the Monarchs gave them a new site on an estate, the former property of the Arab kings, which had a house, mill and orchard. The estate was called "La Almoraba". Once there, finally settled, the first stone of the new monastery was laid in 1519. In 1521, Doña María de Manrique, the second wife and duchess-widow of the Great Captain, asked Charles V to grant her the monastery as a place to bury her husband, herself and their descendants, which the Emperor did in 1523. In exchange, she would have to complete the Chancel and decorate it with a retable, railing and tombs (pantheons or cenotaphs), but only the retable was completed.

The construction of the Church was first commissioned to Jacobo Florentino ("el Indaco") in 1525. He could not complete the project, as he died in 1526. Later, in 1528, the duchess-widow of the Great Captain commissioned the chancel's construction, retable and railing to Diego de Siloé. As he had an argument with the Great Captain's grandson, he only completed part of the church and the doorways of the first cloister.

Previous page:
The Monastery's first cloister, in late Gothic style.

Top:
Detail of the outside of the church from Calle Gran Capitán.

Bottom:
Don Gonzalo Fernández de Córdoba's coat of arms on the outside of the apse.

Left:
*Doorway and main facade of the
church, inside the monastery.*

stands out in this simple decoration, as it has Don Fernando de Córdoba's enormous coat of arms and there is a large cartouche in the upper section held by two women: "Fortitude" (strength) and "Industry" (work), which reads: "Gonzalo Fernandez de Córdoba, great general of the Spaniards and terror of the French and the Turks". It comes as no surprise that this irritated Sebastiani and his Napoleonic soldiers when they read it and, remembering the defeats of Cerignola, Garigliano and Gaeta, they plundered the church and the monastery.

The main facade, now inside the monastery, has three sections. The first contains the door, adorned with two Doric columns on either side. The Penitent St. Jerome, who is missing one hand, is above the door, flanked by four pinnacles. In the saint's other hand he is holding a stone to scourge himself with, and by his side is the lion who accompanied him in the solitude of his hermitage. Hanging on the right are the saint's attributes as a Doctor of the Church. The second section contains the coat of arms of the Catholic Monarchs, their crowned initials and their symbols (the yoke and the arrows). The third has an extremely beautiful window with stained glass that lets light pass through to the choir. On either side of the window are the busts of St. Peter and St. Paul, with cartouches above them with their names. It is all framed by some imaginary animals, such as hippogriffs, characteristic of Siloé.

The tower has four sections. Only the two at the bottom are original. The two top sections were removed by order of the French General Sebastiani to use the stones to build the "Puente Verde" (Green Bridge) over the river Genil.

With the invasion of Napoleon's troops, the monastery was plundered by General Sebastiani, who occupied it with his armies. The Confiscation in 1835 led to the monks being expelled. In 1973 it was returned to the Order and since 1977 these walls, now restored, are inhabited by a community of Hieronymite nuns, who generously open their doors to visitors.

THE OUTSIDE OF THE CHURCH

The outside of the monastery, the part overlooking Calle Gran Capitán, is almost octagonal in shape, with strong buttresses and thick stonework walls. As there is not much decoration, apart from the Great Captain's coats of arms decorating the apse, the sides and the dome, it looks more like a fortress than a church. Perhaps this was deliberate to honour the memory of the great soldier resting here. The lower section of the centre of the apse

Gonzalo Fernández de Córdoba "The Great Captain"

The famous Gonzalo Fernández de Córdoba, the second child of the Count of Aguilar, was born in Montilla (Cordoba) on 1 september 1453. From when he was very young he was the page of Prince Alphonse, the brother of Henry IV of Castile, "the Impotent", and the future Queen Isabella I, who was especially fond of him.

As a soldier, he was involved in the wars of succession for the kingdom of Castile on Isabella and Ferdinand's side and against the nobles who, supported by Portugal, opposed the appointment of Isabella as Queen. His participation in the Battle of "Albuera" (1479), in which Ferdinand defeated the Portuguese, was very noteworthy.

From 1481, he took an active part in the wars for the conquest of the Kingdom of Granada, until the Nasrids surrendered in 1492. The Monarchs rewarded him for his participation in taking Granada with large estates and possessions in this city. Other nobles and soldiers involved were also rewarded with immense possessions for their services. Returning briefly from Italy, he fought in another war in Granadine lands in 1499: the first revolution of the Moriscos in the Alpujarras.

It was his part in the Italian Wars (1495-1504) that gave Gonzalo Fernández de Córdoba fame and legendary status throughout all of Europe and he became known by the nickname of "the Great Captain". This conflict arose when Charles VIII of France entered Naples and deposed Ferdinand II, the King of this Kingdom and a relation of Ferdinand the Catholic. To

Top:
Praying sculpture of Gonzalo Fernández de Córdoba on one of the sides of the chancel.

alleviate this situation, the Catholic King sent his most illustrious general, Gonzalo, who disembarked in Calabria on 26 May 1495. After many mishaps and conflicts, the "treaty of Granada" was signed in secret between the new King of France Louis XII and Ferdinand the Catholic, by which both monarchs divided up the Kingdom of Naples between them.

Nevertheless, France and Spain became enemies again, and Ferdinand the Catholic sent Gonzalo a second time. Once there, he started his triumphant passage. With his famous infantry regiments, called "tercios", he regained Calabria (which he had lost before), defeated the French in the "Battle of Cerignola" in 1503 and he entered Naples defeating the famous French General Bayardo, known as "the gentleman beyond fear and reproach", in 1504. Gonzalo was so generous towards those he had defeated that they called him "kind captain and kind gentleman".

He was appointed viceroy of Naples, but he exceeded his authority by sharing out titles and favours among his officers, as well as ecclesiastical benefits, arguing that he shared them among those who had fought so well and who therefore deserved them. In this year (1504), Queen Isabella, his great protector, died. Ferdinand the Catholic, who seemed to view his great fame with some suspicion, finally asked him for the accounts. The Great Captain was starting to overshadow him in Italian lands and, moreover, the king was short of funds. Ferdinand the Catholic ended up saying: "What does it matter to me if Gonzalo has won a kingdom if he gives it all away before I get my hands on it".

Top:
Praying statue of Doña María de Manrique, the Great Captain's second wife and duchess-widow.

Gonzalo took this complaint extremely disdainfully, and, as he was not a man to joke around, he wanted to teach the treasurers of the kingdom and even the King a lesson and prove who the real debtor was: himself or the Treasury. In an audience before the latter, he began to read out what are known as "the Great Captain's accounts", which are transcribed below as they are one of those curious facts or anecdotes history sometimes rewards us with:

"Two hundred thousand seven hundred and thirty-six ducats and nine reals on monks, nuns and the poor so that they can pray to God for the prosperity of the king's weapons.- A hundred million on pickaxes, spades and mattocks.- A hundred thousand ducats on gunpowder and cannon balls.- Ten thousand ducats on perfumed gloves to preserve the troops from the stench of dead enemies.- A hundred and seventy thousand ducats for repairing and restoring the bells as a result of pealing every day in honour of our new victories over our enemies.- Fifty thousand ducats on brandy for the troops on days of combat.- One and a half million for looking after prisoners and the wounded.- A million for thanksgiving masses and Te Deums in honour of the Almighty.- Seven hundred thousand four hundred and ninety-four ducats on spies.- And finally, a hundred million for the patience lost listening to people asking for accounts from those that have won kingdoms".

All the above, as well as the fact that some courtiers were envious of the Great Captain, meant that the differences between Ferdinand the Catholic and Gonzalo grew, to the extent that the King tried everything in his power to get him out of Naples. Gonzalo, disillusioned by so many cunning arguments used against him, ended up returning to Spain. However, the "astute" King Ferdinand, to iron out the differences between him and the best soldier of his armies, granted him the "estate of Loja" for life. Almost exiled and realising he was dying, Gonzalo Fernández de Córdoba retired to his house in Granada, in the square called Plaza de las Descalzas (there is a commemorative plaque), where he died on the second of December 1515, a month and twenty-three days before the king, who had totally forgotten him, as he had also forgotten Christopher Columbus.

MONASTERY AND CLOISTER

The monastery is accessed via a doorway that is on the right of the church. Above it is the motto of the order: "Honour and Glory to God Alone", the work of Martín Navarrete. The monastery has two cloisters. However, only one of them can be visited, as the other belongs to the secluded area for the nuns and it can only be seen from the railing on the right side of the first cloister (which can be visited), next to the stairs leading to the secluded area. This second cloister is Renaissance in style and Empress Isabella, the wife of Charles V, stayed there in 1526, as she thought that the rooms that had been prepared for her in the Alhambra were too cold. The second section of this cloister and the staircase were razed to the ground by a fire and they were restored between 1965 and 1968.

The first cloister has a beautiful garden in the centre, with a fountain surrounded by orange and lemon trees, cedars, myrtles and aromatic plants that remind us of a Hispano-Muslim garden. The architecture style is late Gothic or Isabelline. The influence of Enrique Egas can be seen in the arches and capitals, although they were designed by an unknown artist. The cloister is formed by a total of thirty-six arches, nine on each side. The inside is decorated with the coats of arms of the Catholic Monarchs and the first archbishop of Granada and hieronymite monk, Fray Hernando de Talavera, Queen Isabella's confessor. It was finished in 1519.

The top part belongs to the secluded area. Above, on one of the sides, between the tower and the dome, there is a wide corridor or "solarium", where those convalescing from

Top:
Detail of the first cloister.
Of the two in the monastery,
it is the only one open to
visitors.

about the "sacristy", which has Cardinal Mendoza's coat of arms above the doorway, is that a Gothic Baby Jesus is kept here, which the Great Captain took with him into battle.

Take a look at the small marble gravestones on the floor. This is where the dead monks were buried, with their abbreviated name engraved on them. They say there are five hundred of them, and as there are so many and the space is so small, they may even have been buried vertically. The final detail to notice is the four boat lanterns in the corners, which lit up the cloister at night.

Left:
Two of the beautiful doorways, by Siloé, embellishing the cloister.

Bottom:
Detail of the cloister's columns.

illnesses were walked and sunbathed. Notice the coat of arms of the Great Captain at one of the ends.

There are seven doorways around the cloister's corridors, all by Siloé. The majority of them lead to the community's rooms, such as "de profundis" "refectory" and "chapter house". The "Ecce Homo" doorway, the first on the left, which leads to a chapel, is perhaps the mot striking. It has reliefs of the St. Johns, St. Peter, St. Paul, St. Gregory and St. Jerome on its arch. The majority of these doorways were designed as chapels of the most noble families in Granada for later burial of their members, such as the families of Bobadilla, Diaz Sánchez Dávila and Ponce de León. However, they were used later by the community for practical purposes.

The "de profundis" room leads to the "refectory" or dining hall, where there is a fountain with the motto "Ave Maria", where the monks washed their hands before going in to eat. The dining hall has continuous brick benches, a pulpit for religious readings during meals and a small fountain in a niche decorated with tiles. The paintings on the walls are by Juan de Sevilla and there is a lovely "Immaculate Conception" by Pedro Atanasio Bocanegra hanging on the end wall. A curious fact

INSIDE THE CHURCH

The church has one nave with a crossing and a chancel with a retable. The nave has two well differentiated parts: *the first*, from the entrance door to the crossing, is Isabelline Gothic style, with a gold and blue ceiling, very much in the style of Enrique Egas and his work in the "Royal Chapel". He, or one of his disciples, probably designed it, since Florentino did not take part in this monastery until 1523. The most outstanding features of its decoration are the paintings on the ceilings and walls. *The second part*, from the crossing to the high altar, is Renaissance style, and it is clearly the work of the master Diego de Siloé.

There are two frescos by Juan de Medina on either side of the entrance door: "Jesus Driving the Merchants from the Temple" and "St. Peter Curing the Cripple". There are angels, seraphs and cherubs between the vault's ribs and archangels on the columns supporting them. All these fresco paintings were done in the 18th century, as were the rest covering the entire church. Some are by unknown artists and others by well-known ones, such as the above-mentioned Juan de Sevilla and Martín de Pineda.

There are four chapels on each side with ribbed vaults inside, the work of Florentino. These chapels contain quite important sculptures, such as "Christ Recumbent" and "Our Lady of Solitude", which are brought out every year in the procession on Good Friday.

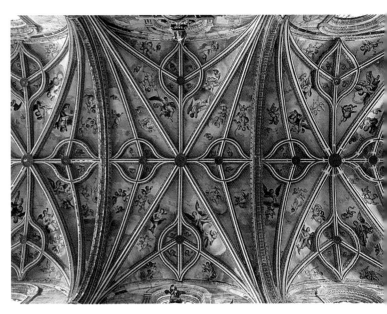

Top:
Ceiling of the church's nave, in Isabelline Gothic style.

The choir is in the top part, where the organ cases are empty and have no pipes. There are also walnut stalls made by Siloé. The paintings are also religious and worth highlighting is "The Triumph of the Eucharist" by Juan de Medina. Unfortunately, not all the stained glass previously covering the large windows has survived and what you can still see today is by Arnao de Vergara.

The work by Siloé starts at **the crossing**, and the style changes from Gothic to the purest Renaissance. It is supported by huge arches, profusely decorated with figures of heroes and heroines of antiquity: Caesar, Hannibal, Pompey, Homer... The reason why these non-religious figures are in a Catholic church is because their exploits were similar to the Great Captain's. The vault is cross-ribbed, decorated with cherubs and busts. It is octagonal in shape with double central braces

and supported by four pendentives, where the Evangelists are located. It is all lit by four circular stained glass windows with the Great Captain's coat of arms.

There are two chapels on either side of the crossing containing the Great Captain's weapons, flanked by "lansquenets" (mercenary soldiers from the Swiss infantry who fought under his orders).

Above them are the seated statues of four virtues, two for each altar. "Faith" and "Hope" are on the left and "Fortitude" and "Justice" are on the opposite side.

Right in front of the staircase leading to the chancel you come across a simple and very deteriorated tombstone made of marble. The mortal remains of Gonzalo Fernández Córdoba lie under it, with a simple inscription in Latin marking the spot: *"Gonzalo Fernández de Córdoba, whose courage earned him the name of the Great Captain. His remains are buried here until they are restored to the perpetual light. His glory is not buried with him".*

In the chancel there is a **large retable**, which is perhaps one, if not the best, of Spanish Renaissance retables. It was commissioned in 1570 and its first creators were: Juan de Aragón, Diego Pesquera, Lázaro de Velasco, Juan Bautista Vázquez, Pablo de Rojas and his then young disciple Juan Martínez Montañés, Pedro de Orea, Pedro de Raxis and Diego de Navas. A whole host of artists who nevertheless managed to turn the retable into a coherent whole.

The retable has four tiers, which rest on a row of reliefs of saints. It is topped by a pediment dominated by the figure of God the Father. As it is so varied and complex, due to the large number of figures represented, this description only refers to the most outstanding features in every tier.

First tier: The Madonna of the Pear is in the central niche. St. Peter and St. Paul are on either side. Next to them are reliefs of the "Birth of Jesus" and the "Adoration of the Magi".

Second tier: The Immaculate Conception is in the centre. At her feet are her parents, St. Joachim and St. Anne. This is the first time in the history of art that a retable has been dedicated to the Virgin. St. John the Baptist and St. John the Evangelist (in the cauldron) and reliefs of the "Incarnation" and "Presentation" are on the sides.

Third tier: It is dominated by the Penitent St. Jerome with the Lion. Christ at the Column and the Ecce Homo are on the sides. This tier is completed with reliefs of the "Arrest of Christ", "Agony in the Garden", "Crucifixion" and a "Pietà".

Fourth tier: There is a "Christ on the Cross" with the Virgin Mary and St. John the Evangelist in the centre and reliefs of "the Ascension" and the "Coming of the Holy Spirit" (Pentecost) on either side. The coats of arms of the Great Captain and his wife, María de Manrique, are in the side sections.

Previous page:
General view of the nave from the high altar.
The choir and the organs are in the background.
Right:
Details of some of the numerous paintings decorating the church's walls.

Left:
High altar and crossing from the central nave. (Described on the previous page).

Top:
Vault of the crossing (Described on page 201).

At the very top of this retable there is a broken pediment with the figures of God the Father and Sts. Justus and Pastor. Above them are the virtues of "Faith", "Hope" and "Charity". Separated from the pediment, and on either side of it, are "Fortitude" and "Temperance".

At the bottom, on either side, are the donors of the monastery, kneeling in prayer: Gonzalo Fernández de Córdoba and his wife. There is a fresco above the figure of the Great Captain representing him receiving the sword to defend the Church from Pope Alexander VI, which is stated in Latin below the painting.

The original sword was here until it was stolen by the French General Sebastiani in 1810. He also looted all the church's treasure when he turned the monastery into barracks and stables: jewellery, the Plateresque railings, which enclosed the chapels, the organ pipes, standards and a vast number of banners won by the Great Captain in his battles (according to Miguel Lafuente Alcántara, there were about seven hundred).

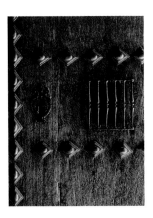

OTHER MONUMENTS

of interest

Royal Hospital, Basilica of San Juan de Dios and Plaza de la Universidad. Three must-sees along the route linking the monasteries of Cartuja and San Jerónimo.

The Royal Hospital

The Catholic Monarchs had founded a first *Hospital Real* (Royal Hospital) in the Alhambra in 1501, whose main purpose was to care for the wounded in the War. Nevertheless, this first hospital was provisional, since the founding monarchs, among other large architectural projects planned for the city, had thought of building a large, definitive hospital for the sick and the destitute. It was decided to locate the building in a place previously occupied by a former Muslim cemetery, just outside the gate called Puerta de Elvira. Work was started in 1511 and it was interrupted soon after and then resumed in 1522, under the management of Juan García de Pradas. It started to operate as a hospital in 1526 and the sick were transferred from the hospital in the Alhambra and put in a small part that had been finished. Later it was a "madhouse" and a hospice.

There is an overlapping of different styles in the building, mainly as a result of how long it took to construct and alterations to adapt it to emerging requirements. The first stage (1511-1522) has left architectural traces of late Gothic style. From 1522, when Juan García de Pradas took charge of the project, the style and architectural elements of the Renaissance began to overlap the former Gothic work. The project came to a standstill at the end of the 16th century, above all because there were no financial resources to continue the work. The most outstanding part built in the 17th century is the facade's doorway, dating from the first third of that century. New alterations were effected in the 18th

Top:
Detail of the large wooden front door.

Bottom:
Main facade of the Royal Hospital.

century, involving the redistribution of the hospital to adapt it to new requirements.

All the building's walls and its main facade are very austere, apart from four Plateresque windows in the top section, by Pradas, and the doorway. The most significant elements of this doorway are: two Corinthian columns on either side of the door in the bottom section; a sculpture of the Madonna and Child with the founding Monarchs praying on either side in the second section. At the very top of the doorway there is St. John's eagle[1], with the Monarchs' coat of arms and their initials, which can be found all over the building, on either side.

The plan is a Greek cross inside a square, with four courtyards in every one of the angles of the cross. Without a doubt, these courtyards are one of the most outstanding elements in the entire complex. Those on the left are the most interesting, especially the first, with five arches on each one of its sides, supported on slender columns and decorated with features referring to the Catholic Monarchs and their grandson, Emperor Charles V. Another of the most striking elements are the ceilings. Those made of wood are the work of the master carpenters Juan de Plasencia and Melchor Arroyo, who was also responsible for the large coffered cupola covering the inside of the dome, which can be seen in this building's beautiful library.

This monument currently houses the central services of the University of Granada and its courtyards and rooms in the crossing are used for holding academic or cultural events of all kinds. It is also the location of several different exhibitions.

Top:
One of the courtyards inside the building.

Bottom:
Detail of one of the courtyard's arches. It is surrounded by royal symbols. The most noticeable is St. John's eagle.

[1]Every Evangelist had a representative symbol: St. Mark a lion, St. Luke a bull, St. Matthew an angel and St. John an eagle. As the Catholic Monarchs worshipped this Saint, they included this eagle as the bearer of their coat of arms. It was included in all the coats of arms of Spain until the Bourbon dynasty took over.

The Basilica of San Juan de Dios

It is consecrated to the Immaculate Conception and dedicated to St. John of God[2]. Construction was started in 1737, under the management of José de Bada, and it was opened for worship in 1759. The style is Baroque, and it is so richly decorated that there is hardly a gap on its walls that is not covered with profuse ornamentation.

Twin belfries stand out in its exterior facade, which are covered by slate roofs. The doorway, designed by José de Bada, is made of marble from Sierra Elvira, and it has two richly worked sections. There are statues of the Archangels St. Raphael and St. Gabriel, by Ramiro Ponce de León, between Corinthian columns on either side of the door in the bottom section. St. John of God, also by Ponce, is in the top section with St. Ildephonsus and the Martyrdom of St. Barbara, by Agustín Vera Moreno, on either side, also between columns. At the very top of the doorway is the figure of God the Father.

Top:
Facade of the Basilica of San Juan de Dios.

Bottom:
Inside the Basilica.

The plan is a Latin cross with chapels at the sides of the nave. All the retables in this church are by José Francisco Guerrero. Alongside the Baroque retables, the paintings decorating the arches, vaults and dome are without a doubt the best feature. The paintings represent Saints, Evangelists, the founders of Religious Orders, the Virtues and scenes of the life of the Virgin Mary and St. John of God. They are

almost all by Sánchez Sarabia, although some of them (such as those of the chapels' arches) are by Tomás Ferrer.

The Chancel's **retable**, by José de Bada and José Francisco Guerrero, is churrigueresque style and it is decorated with gold leaf. The images adorning it are: the Immaculate Conception at the very top, St. Ildephonsus, St. Charles Borromeo, St. Joachim and St. Anne, by Sánchez Sarabia and St. John Nepomucene at the top of the tabernacle, by Ramiro Ponce de León. Before the retable on either side of the Chancel are two large paintings: "The Virgin Mary Appearing to St. John of God" and "Death of St. John of God", which are by Conrado Gianquinto. There is a window in the form of an arch in the central section, which leads to a *camarín* (shrine-chapel). The **camarín** has a great deal of precious materials and mirrors and it is even more richly decorated than the church. There is a tabernacle in the centre and kept inside in a silver urn, decorated by the silversmith Miguel de Guzmán, are the remains of St. John of God. The profuse decoration includes numerous reliquaries with skulls and bones of martyrs, such as St. Felician, whose complete skeleton is kept in an urn. The vault paintings are by Sánchez Sarabia.

There are excellent works of art in the **side chapels,** such as a statue of St. John of God, by Bernardo de Mora, and another of St. Joseph with Child, by José Risueño. The paintings by Pedro Atanasio Bocanegra are worth noting, especially the one of the Immaculate Child between St. Joachim and St. Anne.

There are two small doors at the sides of the retable in the bottom section leading to the **sacristy**, which is also very richly decorated. The most outstanding features of the sacristy are the paintings on the ceiling, which, as in the church, are also by Sarabia. The vestment cases are by Francisco Guerrero.

[2] Juan Ciudad Duarte (St. John of God) was born in March 1495 in Montemor-o-Novo (Portugal). For several reasons, he came to live in Oropesa (Toledo) in Spain. During his first period in this country, he enlisted as a soldier on two occasions, to fight against the French and the Turks. In 1538 he settled in Granada, the city where he found true conversion at the hands of St. John of Avila. His transformation was so radical that

the people viewed him as a madman, and he was interned in the Royal Hospital. His time in hospital was to mark his life and from then on he dedicated all his efforts to the sick and needy. He founded a first hospital in some premises in the street Calle Lucena in Granada, which grew and was then transferred to a larger place. At first he worked alone, but gradually he found other collaborators. His work consisted of caring for and feeding the poor and sick so that they could have a decent life, and begging for them in the streets. He died in March 1550, the victim of pneumonia, which he caught when he dived into the River Genil to try to save a young man from drowning.

Church of San Justo y Pastor in the Plaza de la Universidad.

The Plaza de la Universidad

The Plaza de la Universidad is very central, near the cathedral. It is a secluded square, which, as a result of its beautiful surroundings and the facades of its main buildings, the **Facultad de Derecho** (Faculty of Law) and the **Collegiate Church of San Justo y Pastor** (Sts. Justus and Pastor), is one of the most picturesque parts of the city centre. During term time this square and the streets leading off it are full of students toing and froing with their books and folders, a typical scene in this city. After all, the University of Granada is one of the first founded in Europe and one of the most important in Spain. There is a statue of Emperor Charles V in the middle of the square, as he ordered the creation of a "Literary University" in Granada in 1526, the origin and forerunner of the current one, where Theology, Philosophy, Logic and Grammar were studied.

The **Faculty of Law** building was formerly the property of the Jesuits. Today, the majority of it is a modern construction and it has been greatly altered. All that is left of the former building are two cloisters, the ceiling of the assembly hall (former chapel) and the facade's doorway, dating from the 18th century, with Baroque columns and an image of the Immaculate Conception. This building was the headquarters of the University of Granada from 1769, after the Jesuits were expelled. Before then, and from the founding of the university, the headquarters had been located in what is today known as the *Palacio de la Curia Eclesiástica* (Ecclesiastical Curia Palace), opposite the *Cathedral*. Today it is the Faculty of Law.

The **Collegiate Church of San Justo y Pastor** also belonged to the Jesuits, who built it. Work was started in 1575 and finished around 1621. The tower and the main doorway are later, dating from the middle of the 18th century. The doorway has beautiful reliefs by Vera Moreno. The image crowning it is a St. Ignatius. The building right next to the church is the parish house, and it was part of the former Jesuit College of San Pablo de la Compañía de Jesús.

Inside, the church, with a Latin cross plan, is sober and harmonious. Worth noting is the chancel, with a polychrome gold and black retable, made by Francisco Díaz de Rivero in 1630. He was a Madrilenian carpenter who had previously entered the Order of the Jesuits. It has twisted column-shafts (torsos) with a semicircular recess in the centre, where there is a revolving and mobile tabernacle, whose purpose is to hide and show the Holy Sacrament. At the sides there are reliquaries that are opened during solemnities. The large painting at the top of the retable represents "The Conversion of St. Paul" and it is by Pedro Atanasio Bocanegra, who also painted the others on the walls of the Chancel. There are two images of the martyred child saints Justus and Pastor, who this church is named after. Some of the sculptures and images in the side chapels are quite important and well worth taking a look at.

Top:
Statue of Charles V and doorway of the Church of San Justo y Pastor.

Bottom:
Part of the Square with the doorway of the Faculty of Law in the background.

Other places of interest

The Realejo Quarter

This is one of the oldest and most typical quarters in Granada, covering the slope going down from the Alhambra on the southern side.

This is the oldest quarter in Christian Granada, after the conquest. In Muslim times this was where the Granadine sultans' royal *huertas* (orchards and cultivated fields) were located, stretching down towards the river. As royal is *real* in Spanish, this was the origin of the quarter's name. It covered the slope going down from the Alhambra on the southern side, or Antequeruela[1], and it was connected to the "Mauror" Jewish quarter via the gate of *Bibaxarc* or "Puerta del Sol" (Gate of the Sun) and thus divided into the upper and lower Realejo. In Muslim times the quarter was known as "Rabad-Al-Fajjarin" or the potters' quarter, and it had a *jima* (a small mosque that was usually found in every quarter) called "Abengimara", which the "Casa de los Tiros" was built on, as well as other important buildings.

The main squares and streets with the majority of the monuments are in this popular Granadine quarter are: Campo del Príncipe, Calle Molinos, Plaza de Santo Domingo and Calle Pavaneras.

The heart of this quarter is **Campo del Príncipe** (Prince's Field), a large square at the foot of the Hotel Palace and the Rodríguez Acosta Foundation on the southern side as you come down from the Alhambra. In Muslim times it was called "Albunest" or "Campo de la Lona" (Field of Canvas). There was a cemetery and large huertas and gardens here. The "Cristo de los Favores"

Top:
Cristo de los Favores (Christ of Favours), which the Granadines worship.

Bottom:
Doorway of the Church of San Cecilio.

Right:
The square Campo del Príncipe, dominated by the Cristo de los Favores.

(Christ of Favours), which the Granadines worship, is in this square, and people have congregated here since 1682 every Good Friday at three o'clock in the afternoon to recite the "seven words of Jesus Christ", asking him for three favours. There are two theories about the square's current name: one is that the Granadines gave it this name in honour of the wedding of Prince John (the Catholic Monarchs' only son, 1478-1497) and the other due to the prince's death, as he fell off his horse and died as a result in 1497, a few months after his marriage to Margaret of Austria. (Ref.: *La Alhambra* by Rafael Contreras, page 335).

This square is one of the most picturesque places in Granada, where Granadines and visitors often go for a drink and a typical Granadine "tapa" in one of the bars and *tascas* that have always been here.

The **Church of San Cecilio** (St. Cecilius, the patron of Granada) is in the top part of the *Campo del Príncipe*. Prior to the Arabs, it was the "Jima Alyahud" or "Jewish Synagogue". Worth noting inside the church are an "Our Lady of Bethlehem" by Alonso de Mena and a "St. Peter of Alcantara" by José de Mora. Close by, also in the top part, is the **Convent of St. Catherine of Siena**, dating from the 16th century. The small square called "Placeta de la Puerta del Sol" (Gate of the Sun) is also nearby. This is where the gate with the same name formerly stood, and there is a well preserved **public washhouse dating from the 17th century**, the only one left in Granada.

Another of the most beautiful squares in the Realejo is the "Plaza de Santo Domingo". In the centre there is a bronze statue of the "Venerable Louis of Granada" and it is dominated by perhaps the most emblematic and important monument in the quarter: **the Church of Santo Domingo** (St. Dominic), whose construction was begun in 1512, with a Gothic facade and the coats of arms of the Catholic Monarchs and Charles V. It also has the initials "F" and "Y" standing for Ferdinand and Isabella. It is one of the few churches that has an *espadaña* rather than a bell tower (an *espadaña* is like a bell tower, but it only has one wall, with gaps for the bells). Worth noting inside are: the float of the "Last Supper" and the sculpture of "Our Lady of the Rosary" with its "camarín" (shrine-chapel), an exuberant example of Baroque.

The house known as **Casa de los Girones**, dating from Muslim times (13th century) is very close to here. Apparently

Top:
Church of Santo Domingo, which the square is named after. There is a statue of the Venerable Louis of Granada in the centre.

it belonged to one of Boabdil's sisters and then became the property of the Téllez Girón family, better known as the Duke and Duchess of Osuna. Opposite the Casa de los Girones is the **Casa de los Condes de Gabia** (14th century house of the Count and Countess of Gabia), where there is now a gallery. Also nearby is the **Convent of the Comendadoras de Santiago** (16th century), where the Holy Week float "Agony in the Garden" is kept.

In the lower part of the Realejo, near Santo Domingo, is the **Cuarto Real de Santo Domingo (Royal Residence of St. Dominic)** or **Almanxarra Palace,**

---

[1] It was called Antequeruela because it was colonised by the Arabs who fled Antequera when it was conquered by Ferdinand I of Aragon, known as "the one from Antequera", in 1410.

which was a huerta and residence of the Muslim kings, where they retired during "Ramadan". Worth noting are an entrance arch and a large room, seven metres lengthways, with magnificent tiles, stuccoes and a large wooden *alfarje* (flat panelled roof). Many of its huertas and gardens have disappeared. As there are no Nasrid inscriptions, it is assumed that this building dates from the 13th century.

In Calle Pavaneras[2], one of the main streets in the quarter, is one of the other most singular monuments: the house called **Casa de los Tiros**. This picturesque building belonged to the Rengifo family, who also owned the *Generalife*, then passed on due to marriage to the Granada Venegas. It now belongs to the city and it houses a museum inside. It has a Castrense style facade with muskets and cannons at the top, which is where the name "tiros" (shots) comes from in Spanish. Five figures decorate the facade: Jason, Mercury, Hector, Theseus and Hercules. Above the door there is a sword over a heart, which represent the motto of the Venegas family: "the heart rules". Worth noting inside is the Caroline style *Golden Room* with a ceiling decorated with portraits and legends of Spanish heroes and noblemen. The rest is dedicated to famous men and women from Granada, such as Washington Irving and Eugenia de Montijo. Next to it is the **Real Cancillería** (Royal Chancellery) where the brilliant Granadine theologian Padre Suárez was born (1548). That is why the secluded square opposite is called Plaza del Padre Suárez. The secluded square Plaza del Padre Suárez opens up in this part of Calle Pavaneras. This is the location of the **Palace of the Condes de Villa Alegre**, nowadays a Mercedarian school (Order of Our Lady of Mercy). The **House of the Marqueses de Casablanca** (16th? century) is also nearby.

[2] The name "Pavaneras" comes from the fact that "pavanas" were made in this street. Pavanas were a garment women wore around their necks and on their shoulders.

On the whole page:
The square Plaza del Padre Suárez.
Facade of the house called
Casa de los Tiros, which houses
an interesting museum.
Ceiling of the "Golden Room"
in the Casa de los Tiros.

From Carrera del Genil to the riverbank

This is the location of the Basílica of Nuestra Señora de las Angustias, the well-loved patron of the city of Granada.

This is one of the most traditional places in Granada, one of the Granadines' favourites, since this is where the **Basilica of Nuestra Señora de las Angustias** (Our Lady of Sorrows, the patron of this city) stands. In this area, at the end of the street, in a place today called the Humilladero, there was a chapel dedicated to St. Ursula and St. Susanna, where a panel was worshipped. It was donated by Queen Isabella the Catholic and represented "the Fifth Sorrow of Our Lady", a painting by Francisco Chacón (15th century). Such was the devotion inspired by the painting that a Brotherhood was formed in 1545 to worship it. The Brotherhood grew to such an extent that a small church was built in 1567 and turned into an independent parish in 1610. A different image was worshipped in this new place to the primitive panel. As this church became too small in the end, construction of the current one was begun in 1663, next to the previous one.

Twin towers stand out in its facade. The image of the Virgin Mary holding the body of her son, in the niche above the door is by Mora. Inside the style is Baroque. Most worth noting are the following: The images of the twelve Apostles, carved by Duque Cornejo (1714-18), the Chancel, which has a marble Baroque retable, by Marcos Fernández Raya, the lovely *camarín* (shrine-chapel), also made of marble, and lastly, the image of Our Lady of Sorrows, dating from the end of the 16th century, which has had later transformations: Christ recumbent, the back cross and the rich clothes were added and the arms and hands were separated from her body. This image goes

On the whole page:
View of the River Genil and the Violón gardens.
Basilica of Nuestra Señora de las Angustias.
Carrera del Genil boulevard.

through the streets of Granada in a procession every year on the last Sunday in September.

Paseo del Salón is at the end of this street with **Paseo de la Bomba** a little further on. Parallel to these streets are some beautiful gardens overlooking the **River Genil**, which starts in the Sierra Nevada and enters the city here.

The Carmen de los Mártires

The romanticism pervading its gardens, raised above the city, on the same hill as the Alhambra, make this an idyllic place.

Top left:
Carmen de los Mártires Palace, built in the second half of the 19th century.

Top right:
Detail of the fountain in the Francés (French) Garden.

Bottom:
The palace's pond.

This is one of the most idyllic and beautiful places in this city, in the vicinity of the Alhambra, so if you can and you have some time, you should visit it. It gets its name (House of the Martyrs) because apparently some Christians were martyred here when the Muslims were ruling. After the conquest, the Catholic Monarchs had a small chapel built here and later the Discalced Carmelite Order built a monastery where St. John of the Cross lived and was the prior. The cypress, which, according to legend, this saint planted, and under which he wrote his book: "Dark Night of the Soul", is still standing in the gardens.

The monastery was destroyed in the 19th century and the estate was passed on to an eminent family who built the palace standing today. It currently belongs to the City Council, which rehabilitated the gardens. The romanticism pervading this place, raised above the city on the same hill as the Alhambra, is without a doubt worth experiencing.

Museums and House-Museums

Granada Fine Arts Museum: Located in the top section of the Palace of Charles V (Alhambra). It houses an important collection of paintings and sculptures dating from the 16th century to the avant-garde movements at the beginning of the 20th century. The most outstanding part of the collection is based on the "Granada school".

Alhambra Museum: Located on the bottom floor of the Palace of Charles V (Alhambra). This museum is a must for anyone wishing to find out more about the Alhambra and the different stages of Hispano-Muslim art, especially the Nasrid period.

Archaeological Museum: Located in the Casa de Castril Palace, Carrera del Darro 41, in Lower Albaycin. This important collection, with exhibits ranging from the Palaeolithic to the Nasrid period, helps us to understand the different cultures that lived in the Province of Granada.

Casa de los Tiros Museum: Very central, in the typical Realejo quarter, Calle Pavaneras 19. The museum is named after the house where it is located, which was built in the 16th century. It is difficult to classify this museum as its exhibits are so diverse. It is structured into extremely interesting rooms with local themes: the landscape, orientalism, travellers, industrial arts and *costumbrismo* (depiction of everyday customs).

Museum of the Rodríguez Acosta Foundation: The headquarters of the Museum and the Foundation are in the carmen (a house with an orchard) that José María Rodríguez Acosta (an important Granadine painter, 1878-1947, born into a famous banking family) had built between 1916 and 1930 in the street called Callejón Niños del Royo at number 8. The building and its gardens are one of the most remarkable and beautiful areas in this city, in the surroundings of the Alhambra. The foundation's important collection of items and works of art increased with the incorporation of the Gómez Moreno Institute, which is in the same complex and connected with the gardens. Extremely valuable archaeological collections, paintings and sculptures, etc., are on display in the Foundation and the Institute.

Manuel de Falla House-Museum: Antequeruela Alta 11. Located in the secluded carmen where this universal Spanish musician and composer lived from 1921 to 1939, which was when he had to leave Spain never to return again. The house and its furnishings have been kept just as the artist left them. It also houses an important selection of documents and personal objects.

Federico García Lorca House-Museum: A visit to Granada is a must for whoever wishes to discover the surroundings that had an influence on this Granadine poet and playwright of international renown. The first stop is the **Federico García Lorca House-Museum** located in Fuente Vaqueros, a few kilometres from the capital of the province, in the heart of the Vega (fertile plain) of Granada. The **House-Museum of the Huerta de San Vicente**, the estate owned by the poet's family, is in the Federico García Lorca park in Granada. This is where he lived between 1926 and 1936, the year when he died. The house has been kept just as it was when the family lived there, and some rooms have been arranged to display the poet's drawings, manuscripts and photographs.

José Guerrero Art Centre: Calle Oficios in the heart of the city. The centre's aim is to preserve and promote the work of José Guerrero (1914-1999), a Granadine painter whose work can be seen in the most important Spanish contemporary art museums. But above all, it is also used as an exhibition centre to spread awareness of work by both local and international contemporary and avant-garde artists.

Science Park: Avenida del Mediterráneo. Interactive science museum where visitors can experiment with different physical phenomena in the Biosphere, Perception, Planetarium, Explore and Eureka rooms. Also on offer are interesting thematic exhibitions throughout the year.

The Province

Map of the province

The Alpujarra

Sierra Nevada

The Coast

The Poniente Granadino

The regions of Guadix and the Altiplano

THE PROVINCE OF GRANADA:
"A SMALL CONTINENT" WAITING TO BE DISCOVERED

Jaén

Huéscar

Córdoba

A-330

Altiplano

Guadix
y
Marquesado

Baza

Montefrío   Moclín   Iznalloz   La Calahorra

N-432

A-335   A-44   A-92   Guadix

Zagra

Loja   Granada

A-92

El Poniente   Sierra
Nevada

A-335

Alhama

A-44   La Alpujarra

Órgiva

A-346

Málaga   La Costa

Almuñecar   Motril

© Taller de la Alfaguarilla

The historical legacy of the province of Granada, as well as its rich landscape and diversity of climate (there are five different microclimates here), is something like a "miniature continent". In just 13,000 square kilometres and in less than two hours, you can go from a height of 3,000 metres, snow and the alpine climate of the **Sierra Nevada**, to the subtropical and warm climate of the coastal beaches. From the mountainous and green scenery of the towns in the **Alpujarra**, to the desert and almost lunar landscapes of the **Guadix** and **Altiplano** (High Plateau) regions. Many of the towns still have architectural remains of their Arab past and of the Christian colonising reconstruction after the conquest, such as those in the **Poniente Granadino** (Granadine West) region, the last frontier of the Nasrid Kingdom in Granada. The province's beauty has been recognised with five natural parks, and one of them, the Sierra Nevada, is also a National Park. The countryside and the small towns and villages dotted around it make this province a favourite destination for nature and rural tourism lovers.

The last pages of this book aim to give you an idea of what these places are like, so that, if you have time, you can visit some of them. Because, besides the Alhambra or the Cathedral, or the many other parts of this beautiful city, the province of Granada is a place dreams are made of.

The Alpujarra

The beauty of this region's landscape, the peculiar architecture of its towns and its legends attracted travellers from all over the world, making it truly universal.

This is the topmost rural region in the province of Granada, part of which is in the province of Almeria. Located on the southern side of the Sierra Nevada, the majority of it is within the Natural Park. There is an extensive area formed by thirty-two municipal districts, which, due to its architecture, landscape and historical legacy, is one of the most picturesque places in the entire province and about which the most has been written.

If there is one thing that distinguishes the Alpujarra, it is the peculiar landscape that shapes the architecture of its towns: whitewashed houses, built on the slope, one above the other in terraces, with their typical flat roofs made of slate and launa with numerous whitewashed chimneys. "Launa" is a clay from this area used to build houses. When it is mixed with water, it becomes waterproof. All the oldest parts of the towns look like each other, regardless of whether they attract more tourists or not. Steep narrow streets made of stone covered by "tinaos"(open porches) with wooden beams, balconies full of flowers and a surprising view at every turn.

On the whole page:
- The towns of Bubión and Capileira in the Barranco de Poqueira ravine.
- A typical chimney. - Balcony of flowers in Capileira.
- Typical whitewashed facade in Capileira.

On the whole page:
- *Trevélez, the highest town in Spain. - Autumn colours.*
- *River Trevélez. - Orchards in autumn in the Alpujarra.*
- *The "Fuente Agria" area in the town of Pórtugos.*

This style of construction is the most obvious mark left by the Muslims on these towns. They not only inhabited these lands for eight centuries prior to the Christian conquest, but for nearly a century after it as well. When the Catholic Monarchs took Granada, many Moors took refuge here, in the shelter of its crested mountains, and years later they were involved in a fierce uprising against the Christians: the "War of the Alpujarras". After the War, in the reign of Philip II, the Moors were expelled forever and these lands became very underpopulated.

From Granada it is accessed via the dual carriageway going to the coast (A-44, in the direction of Motril), taking the signposted turning to the Alpujarra. We will only refer to the best known places on these pages. However, if you have more than one day, it would be better to venture into this territory to discover these other less visited spots where it seems that time has stood still. The first town we come to is **Lanjarón**, the natural gate of the Alpujarra, famous for its spa and medicinal water and with the best infrastructures. The finest and most well-known place in the entire Alpujarra is the ravine called the **Barranco de Poqueira**, with three towns built on its sides. They are the best preserved and have many country houses and other accommodation to offer: **Pampaneira**, **Bubión** and **Capileira**. Other towns very nearby that are a must to visit are **Mecina-Fondales**, **Ferreirola**, **Atalbéitar** or **Pórtugos**, the latter is known for its bitter water source. You should not leave the Alpujarra without going to

Trevélez, the highest town in Spain, at an altitude of 1,700 metres. Famous for its hams and their quality, it is also one of the most visited with the best accommodation and restaurants.

If you can spend more than one day here, you must go beyond Trevélez. Discover these other towns dotted on the slopes that the road goes through: **Juviles**, **Bérchules**, **Mecina Bombarón**… Even further along you come to the **Sierra de la Contraviesa**, further south and nearer the coast. The landscape changes completely, slopes covered in almond trees and vines where the grapes that produce this area's wine grow. The towns of the Contraviesa are perhaps not as well known.

The sensation you get when you first come to the Alpujarra is that it is a place to return to. The beauty of the landscape, its towns, its customs and the way of life of its peoples, means that it is unspoilt and untouched by the passing years.

On the whole page:
The different close-ups
and places in the Alpujarra
shown here are examples of its
picturesque architecture,
the legacy of this land's
Arab past.

Sierra Nevada

This sierra contains the highest mountains on the Iberian Peninsula, with sixteen peaks over 3,000 m high.

The Sierra Nevada Natural and National Park is mainly in the province of Granada, but it also covers Almeria, to a lesser extent. The highest peaks on the Iberian Peninsula are to be found in this sierra, with sixteen over 3,000 metres high. The best known are: **Mulhacén**, the highest on the peninsula, with a height of 3,482 metres; **Veleta** with 3,396 m and **Alcazaba** with 3,364 m. The wealth of its flora and fauna resulted in it being declared a Biosphere Reserve in 1986. In addition it was declared a Natural Park in 1989 and a National Park in 1999.

The most well-known part of the Sierra Nevada is its **Ski Resort**, the most southern in Europe and for many the best in Spain. The fact of the matter is that the exceptional location of this resort gives it a set of qualities that are very difficult to compete with: thirty kilometres from Granada, one of the cities with the best monuments in Europe, and a hundred from the coast, so you can go from snow to sea in less than two hours. This very southern location, combined with its altitude, also make it the resort that has the most days of sun in the whole

On the whole page:
- Veleta Peak (altitude 3,396 m). - North faces in the Sierra Nevada.
- Spanish wild goat. - Primavera amarilla ("yellow spring", a local species).
- Ring ouzel.

of Europe and one of the ones that has the longest snow season, from the end of November to the beginning of May. As a result of its infrastructures, quality of the pistes, mechanical equipment, accommodation and places to spend time when you are not skiing, it is also an exceptional resort. But alongside the good climate, what sets the Sierra Nevada apart from the rest of the resorts, its greatest appeal, above all for younger people, is its après-ski options: bars and restaurants with terraces full of skiers and non-skiers sunbathing, all kinds of shops and pubs and discotheques where the night continues into the early hours of the morning.

On the whole page:
- Tajos de la Virgen.
- Middle mountain area with the Alcazaba in the background.
- General view of the Ski Resort, dominated by Veleta peak, the emblem of this mountain range.

On the whole page:
- Sunset over Boca de la Pescá.
- Alcazaba (3364 m) and Mulhacén
(3482 m). - Cortijo del Hornillo.
- A local species peeping through stone in
the upper mountains. - Gentiana verna
(spring gentian).

However, the best part of the Sierra Nevada is its landscape's beauty and diversity. Given the Park's varied climate and difference in altitudes, its scenery goes from the dense greenery and trees of the lower and middle mountains, to the small alpine vegetation, with massifs covered by slate and the low bushes of the upper mountains. The special climate conditions mean that there are over sixty plant species here that are endemic, unique and exclusive to these parts, the majority of them on the highest slopes. Of the 8,000 species catalogued for the entire peninsula, 2,100 grow in the Sierra Nevada. It is also rich in the variety of fauna living on the massif: more than sixty types of birds, ranging from the griffon vulture or the golden eagle, the largest, to other smaller ones, such as the alpine accentor, the ring ouzel and the rock thrush. Among the mammals are: moles, foxes, weasels, badgers and the queen of these peaks, the Spanish wild goat.

In the spring and summer months, with the thaw, the snow starts to disappear from the highest peaks, the gullies start to fill with streams of water and the many lakes and pools to be found in this sierra appear: Río Seco, Mosca, Vacares, Aguas Verdes, Caldera... Green meadows covered in sheep and small flowers of many different colours also appear. This is the best time to visit this part of the upper sierra, when spring is well underway and in the summer months. On the southern side the gradients are not too steep, so the climb is smooth and simple. The northern face is much more abrupt and precipitous. In summer, some of the accommodation at the Ski Resort is open, but there are also campsites and rural hotels in the towns in the area. The peace and quiet of these places, the mild climate and the beauty of these peaks, in the summer when the snow has melted, make this a privileged spot for trekking and other sports and leisure activities related to nature.

The Coast

Known locally as the Tropical Coast, its scenery alternates between busy crowded beaches and quieter, more deserted beaches.

The Province of Granada has more than a hundred kilometres of coastline, located between the Coast of Malaga and the Coast of Almeria. It is known locally as the **Tropical Coast**, since due to its special microclimate, with over three hundred days of sun per year and an average annual temperature of twenty degrees centigrade, it is the ideal place to grow tropical fruit and vegetables. The scenery alternates between the busy crowded beaches of the most visited towns and other quieter, more deserted beaches. It is accessed from Granada along the A-44 dual carriageway, direction Motril, at about seventy kilometres.

The most visited and well-known towns are: *Almuñécar, Salobreña* and *Motril*. **Almuñécar** was founded by the Phoenicians, who called it "Sexi". It was also inhabited by the Romans and the Arabs. Its beaches are the most crowded and touristic along the entire coast. The old quarter of the town is crowned by the Castle of San Miguel (St. Michael), an Arab fortress altered in the 16th century. Next to Almuñécar, and

On the whole page:
- Cliffs on the Granadine coast. - Boats moored in the Marina del Este.
- Fishermen returning to the beach. - La Herradura bay.
- Velilla beach. - Cotobro walkway.

belonging to the same municipal district, is the small town of **La Herradura**, nestling around a beautiful bay. It has one of the cleanest and richest seabeds of the entire Mediterranean coast. **Salobreña**, also founded by the Phoenicians –they called it "Salambina"- is a picture postcard coastal town: a hill covered in white houses, topped by a castle rising up above the green crops of the fertile plain surrounding it. Its Arab fortress, dating from the 13th century, was used by the Nasrid kings as a summer residence and also as a prison, where other members of the royal family, who had fallen into disgrace or had been dethroned, were imprisoned. **Motril** is the second largest population centre in the whole province, with the most important fishing and commercial port of the entire Granadine coast.

To the east of Motril are the towns of the *Eastern Tropical Coast*: **Castell del Ferro**, **Castillo de los Baños**, **la Mamola**, **Melicena** and **la Rábita**, small towns with much quieter and more deserted beaches and coves, containing remains of castles and towers. The Muslims built this type of military construction along the entire coast of Al-Ándalus, since they were always under threat from other tribes and peoples from the North of Africa, who wanted their dominions. This brief description should also include a mention of some other towns of the interior, which are very near the coast, but which still have the charm and the peace and quiet of the surrounding sierras: **Molvízar**, **Ítrabo**, **Jete**, **Otívar**...

The Poniente Granadino

As the "last frontier of Al-Ándalus", these lands were the dividing line between the territories ruled by the Christians and the Nasrid kingdom of Granada.

On the whole page:
- Panoramic view of Montefrío, one of the most beautiful towns in Andalusia.
- Montefrío, with the circular church of Encarnación in the foreground.
- Cereal fields in the Poniente.

This region is located in the most western part of the province, on the border with the provinces of Malaga, Cordoba and Jaen. These lands were the frontier area marking the dividing line between the territories ruled by the Christians and the Nasrid kingdom of Granada, in the last period of its existence. As the "last frontier of Al-Ándalus", the settlements in the west had their own identity, located in high areas around a castle or watchtower, in strategic positions to defend the kingdom and with numerous examples of military architecture.

Moclín, **Íllora**, **Montefrío**, **Zafra**, **Loja** and **Alhama de Granada** are no doubt the towns that have the most and the best monumental remains of this historical past. But it is not only the wealth of monuments that makes this region attractive, it is also the beauty of the landscape you will come across on driving along these quiet secondary roads linking the towns together. Carefully ploughed fields, areas of olives and cereals, are an indication of the measured country life led in these lands.

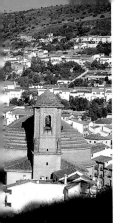

There are two itineraries, both less than an hour from Granada and both with extremely good examples of the wealth of monuments and nature of this "last frontier of Al-Ándalus". The first, in the direction of Cordoba, leads us to **Montefrío**, one of the most beautiful towns in Andalusia. It is crowned by the Church of the Villa (Town) (16th century), which the Catholic Monarchs had built on the remains of a former Arab fortress. It has other two buildings of interest: the Church of the Encarnación (Incarnation) (18th century) and the Church of the Convento de San Antonio (Convent of St. Anthony) (18th century). Also worth visiting are other nearby towns, such as **Moclín**, **Íllora** or **Zafra**, all with remains of former castles.

The second itinerary, in the direction of Malaga, takes us to **Alhama de Granada**, overlooking a spectacular gorge. Known for its thermal baths, used by the Arabs since the 12th century, it has important artistic monuments: the Churches of Encarnación (Incarnation) and Carmen (Our Lady of Mount Carmel) (15th to 16th centuries); the Casa de la Inquisición (House of the Inquisition); the Pósito, a Jewish synagogue until the 13th century and a silo for grain in medieval times; and the Hospital de la Reina (Queen's Hospital) (15th century).

On the whole page:
- Moclín Castle,
at the top of the town.
- Ploughed field between
Moclín and Montefrío.
- Close-up of wheat.
- Remains of the ramparts
of Moclín Castle.
- Alhama de Granada,
with its houses hanging
over the gorge.

The regions of Guadix and the Altiplano

A land of contrasts in the north-east of the province, where the arid desert landscape mixes with fertile plains and mountainous sierras.

This is an extremely large area covering the north-east of the province of Granada, a land of huge contrasts, where the arid desert landscape mixes with fertile plains and the mountainous sierras surrounding them. This vast area is formed by two large regions: "**The region of Guadix y Marquesado del Zenete**" and "**the region of the Altiplano**" (High Plateau). The clayey composition of most of the soil has encouraged the existence of cave houses, a typical and distinct home in this area.

At the moment, many of them are used as rural accommodation.

The capital of the first of these regions is **Guadix**, the second city with important monuments in the entire province of Granada. Among its most important monuments are: the Alcazaba (fortress), dating from Muslim times in the 10th and 11th century; the Cathedral, the city's symbol, built on the remains of the main mosque, with architectural elements in a Gothic, Renaissance

and Baroque style. It also has a good number of churches and palatial buildings. Especially worth mentioning is the square called Plaza de la Constitución (16th-17th centuries), declared a historic and artistic site. There is another important monument in the region of Guadix y Marquesado del Zenete, the Castle of La Calahorra, which was built at the beginning of the 16th century. The exterior aspect of a military fortress is combined with an impeccable Renaissance style inside. It can be visited after contacting the family looking after it, since it is privately owned.

The other region in the north-east of the province, the region of the Altiplano, has the city of **Baza** as its most important population centre. Among its monuments are: the Baths in the Jewish quarter and the Alcazaba (fortress), which are Arab monuments; the Co-cathedral of Santa María de la Encarnación (St. Mary of the Incarnation), which is late Gothic style; churches such as Merced (Our Lady of Mercy), Santiago (St. James) and Presentación (Presentation); convents such as Santo Domingo (St. Dominic) or San Jerónimo (St. Jerome) and the Palace of Enriquez. One of this area's greatest virtues is the natural

wealth and beauty of the sierras surrounding it: the **Sierra de Baza** and the **Sierra de Castril** (natural parks), the **Sierra de Sagra** and the **Sierra de Orce**, which make it an excellent place for hiking and rural tourism. The rivers and the green vegetation running through them contrast with the arid landscape of the plain, where there was a huge lake millions of years ago.

On both pages:
- The clayey arid landscape around Guadix.
- Chimney of a cave.
- Almond trees in flower in the Marquesado, with the Sierra Nevada in the background.
- Negratín reservoir, one of the largest in Andalusia.
- A house cave, the most typical and characteristic construction in this environment.
- La Calahorra Castle.
- Guadix Cathedral, this city's symbol, built on the remains of the Main Mosque.